The Complete Book of

POLYMER CLAY

The Complete Book of
POLYMER CLAY

Step-by-Step Instructions ❖ Original Projects ❖ Inspirational Gallery

LISA PAVELKA

award-winning author of *Polymer Clay Extravaganza*

The Taunton Press

The Taunton Press
Inspiration for hands-on living®

The Taunton Press, Inc., 63 South Main Street, PO Box 5506, Newtown, CT 06470-5506
e-mail: tp@taunton.com

Editor: Erica Sanders-Foege
Copy editor: Betty Christiansen
Indexer: Lynda Stannard
Cover design: Teresa Fernandes
Interior design & layout: Susan Fazekas
Illustrator: Susan Fazekas
Cover Photographer: Front cover: © Zach DeSart; Back cover: © Lisa Pavelka, Author photo: © Allen Pavelka
Photographer: All interior photos © Lisa Pavelka with the exception of photos on pp. 12, 17, 19 (bottom), 21, 22, 24 (top and bottom),
25 (left), 36, 44, 62, 72, 80, 87 (bottom right), 90, 100, 110, 103 (top), 119 (left), 124, 138, 148, 158 (top left, top right, middle right, bottom left),
182, 189, 200 (right), 190 (bottom right), 191 (bottom), 193 (left), 197 (top right), 205 (bottom) © Zach DeSart; p. 190 (left) © Ashley Studios;
pp. 192 (top left) and 199 © Lynne Ann Schwarzenberg; p. 196 (right) © George Post; p. 197 (bottom right) © Hadas Cohen; pp. 198 (bottom)
and 202 © Robert Diamante; p. 205 (top right) © Melanie West; p. 206 (top right) © Meg Marchiando; p. 207 (top left) © Bernard Wolf

Library of Congress Cataloging-in-Publication Data

Pavelka, Lisa, 1960-
  The complete book of polymer clay / Lisa Pavelka.
      p. cm.
   Includes index.
   ISBN 978-1-60085-128-5
   1. Polymer clay craft. I. Title.
   TT297.P3296 2010
   738.1'2--dc22

                                          2009042430

Printed in the United States of America
10 9 8 7 6 5 4 3 2 1

The following names/manufacturers appearing in The Complete Book of Polymer Clay are trademarks:
AMACO® Rub 'n Buff®, Ancient Page™, Angelina® Fiber, Armor All®, Cernit®, Creative Options®, CRYSTALLIZED™–Swarovski Elements, FIMO®,
Formica®, Fun Wire™, Future®, Grandma's Secret Rubber Stamp Cleaner®, Hotfix®, Kato
Liquid Polyclay™, Kato Polyclay™, Lisa Pavelka Magic-Glos™, Lisa Pavelka Poly Bonder™, Makin's Clay®, Microsoft®, Mylar®, Photoshop®, Prēmo!
Sculpey®, Ranger Perfect Pearls™, Sculpey®, Sculpey III®, Silly Putty®, Speedball®,
Staedtler® ergosoft®, STP® Son-of-a-Gun!®, Studio™ by Sculpey, Super Sculpey®, Swarovski®, Teflon®, 3M®, Varathane®

To my dear friends Haley and Lisa, who have my back like no other!
And to the beloved memory of Tupper, a constant
companion who gave nothing but love.

acknowledgments

All the hard work, talent, and determination in the world will not lead a person to success without the help of others. There are so many people to thank for their help and support in writing this book and in my own personal creative voyage.

To Allen, my best friend; the most wonderful kids in the world, Jeremiah, Nick, Dani, and Anne; my extraordinary mother, Karoline Freed Biggs Hilt; my amazing stepfather Howard Hilt; my incredibly talented and funny brother, David; and his equally astounding and lovely wife, Betsy. Your belief in me means the world!

Tremendous gratitude to all of the folks at The Taunton Press, especially my fabulous editor Erica Sanders-Foege and Katy Binder, photo editor.

To my friends at JHB: Jay Barr for your faith in my vision; Lisa Lambright, you amaze me like no other! To Barbara "B Barr" and Gen Ferguson; everything you do is magic! Thanks, Ingrid Chermet, for taking me global!

I appreciate the support and friendship of too many people to mention in the space allotted, but here's a start: My friends at CRYSTALLIZED™–*Swarovski Elements*: Nicole Harper, Nick Regine, Rebecca Whittaker; AMACO and Dawn Sandoe; my Art Clay World compatriots Katie Baum and Jackie Trudy; Anne Huizenga and Ruth Keeson at *Polymer CAFÉ Magazine*; Pam Hawkins and my friends at All American Crafts.

I owe a huge debt of gratitude to Miss Carol Duvall; your support, friendship, graciousness, and generosity are treasures.

Everlasting appreciation to dear friends and creative compadres who've inspired and supported me: my soul sisters to whom this book is dedicated, Linda Steiner, Sue Sullivan, Haley Hertz, Sally Finnegan, Laura "Timmy" Timmons, Kristal Wick, Michele Sutter, Glennis Peterson, Ellie Hitchcock, Kelly and Dan Sweeney. If only I had room to list all my other clay and creative friends, but that would be a book unto itself.

Hugs and thanks to my "MJ" Girlfriends Barbara Berg, Laura Bloch, Lynne Fletcher, Laura, Cheryl Rozensweig, Debbi Sherwood, and Gayle Weckstein, and the "goils" of the Las Vegas Polymer Clay Guild who are too numerous to list.

Last, a huge thanks to the artists who generously submitted their artwork for use in the gallery of this book. I am in awe of your talent.

—Lisa Pavelka

contents

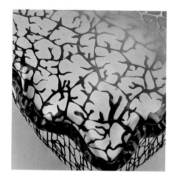

Introduction 2

CHAPTER ONE

Polymer Clay Essentials 6

A Brief History of the Medium 7
Types of Polymer Clay 8
Liquid Clay 10
Safety First 12
Work Surfaces 12
Clay Conditioning and Handling 12
Baking 13
Clay Storage 14
Color Basics 16
Color Recipes 18
Finishing 19

CHAPTER TWO

Tools and Accessories 22

Tools 23
Clay Forming 25
Adhesives 28
Cutting and Shaping Tools 29
Textures 32
Inclusions and Surface Treatments 32
Finishes 35

CHAPTER THREE

Skinner Blending 36

Basic Skinner Blending 39
Multiple-Color Skinner Blending 41
Creating Surface Sheets 42
Gradient Loaves 43
Ribbons 43

CHAPTER FOUR

Millefiori Caning 44

Striped Jelly-Roll Canes 51
Leaf Canes 52
Flower Canes 54
Gradient Checkerboard Canes 56
Gradient Heart Canes 57
Smoosh Canes 57
Junk Canes 60

CHAPTER FIVE

Image Transfers 62

Waterslide Transfers 64
Custom Inkjet Transfers 66
Preprinted Waterslide Transfers 67
Stamps as Transfers 67
Liquid Clay Transfers 68
Toner-Based Transfers 69
Coloring Toner Transfers 70
Deli Paper Transfers 71

CHAPTER SIX

Mokumé Gané 72

Stamped Mokumé Gané 74
Bladed Mokumé Gané 76
Indented Mokumé Gané 77
Folded Mokumé Gané 78
Rolled Mokumé Gané 78

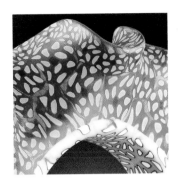

CHAPTER SEVEN

◎ Mica Shift Effects 80

Mica Shift Surface and
Border Treatments 84

Mica Shift Checkerboard Cane 85

Embossed Mica Shifting 86

Mosaic Mica Shifting 87

Wood-Grain Mica Shifting 88

CHAPTER EIGHT

◎ Leaf and Foiling Effects 90

Metal Leafing 92

Polymer Clay Foil 93

Applying Foil 94

Foil Textures and Dimensions 96

Foil Pattern Resists 97

The Pavelka Peel 98

CHAPTER NINE

◎ Faux Effects 100

Faux Opal 102

Faux Turquoise 103

Faux Raku 104

Faux Ivory 106

Faux Cinnabar 108

Faux Rust 108

CHAPTER TEN

◎ Stamping 110

Basic Sutton Slice Sheet 115

Advanced Sutton Slice Concepts 118

Textile Effect 121

Faux Tapestry 122

Additional Embossed-Clay Effects 122

CHAPTER ELEVEN

◎ Assembly, Formation,
and Structure 124

Three-Step Mosaics 126

Carving 129

Hollow Forms 130

Pillow Forms 131

Puff Forms 131

Nontwist Suspension Method
for Hanging Puff Forms 132

Flowers 133

Ribbon Roses 133

Layered Roses 134

Cutter Boxes 135

Stencil Frames 137

CHAPTER TWELVE

◎ Surface Treatments 138

Marbling 140

Barber Pole Striping 141

Border Treatments 142

Stencil Gané 143

Silk Screening 144

Granulars 146

CHAPTER THIRTEEN

◎ Finishing Touches
and Final Thoughts 148

Scrap Clay 150

Additional Thoughts on Molding 151

Leafing Pens 152

Suspending Clay 152

Tube Attachments 152

Fold-Over Bails 154

Connecting Pieces to Jump Rings 156

Fancy or Coil-Wrapped Loops 157

CHAPTER FOURTEEN

◎ Projects to Make 158

Suspended Crystal Pendant 160

Magic Mirror 164

Swirly Whirly Faux Art
Glass Bracelet 168

Faux Dichroic Shield Pendant 172

Image Transfer Inro Amulet 176

Sutton Slice "About Face" Case 182

CHAPTER FIFTEEN

◎ Gallery of
Polymer Clay Art 188

Appendix I: Troubleshooting for
Polymer Clay 208

Appendix II: Glossary of Polymer
Clay Terms 211

Resource Guide 216

Index 219

introduction

begin this book with a bit of a disclaimer. Considering the hundreds of techniques and applications for polymer clay, those known and those yet to be discovered, it would be impossible to offer the truly "complete" book of clay. As a part of a book series, this book is offered to provide a comprehensive collection of most of the commonly known and universal techniques and applications for polymer clay, including a few of my own.

One would be hard pressed to work with an artistic medium as dynamic, versatile, and forgiving as polymer clay. Developed in the 1930s in Germany, this incredible material has undergone numerous changes over the course of its evolution. New formulations, new colors, and even liquid versions have appeared over the years. Without a doubt, this evolutionary process will continue to move forward, offering new techniques and applications.

The popularity of polymer clay began to grow exponentially after the introduction of individually colored clays in the 1980s. The ongoing improvements of clay formulas plus the introduction of new tools and accessories (including those that have crossover applications for clay) also continue to build public awareness of the medium and its versatility.

My adventures in clay began in the late 1980s, while searching for an artistic medium that would be safe to work with while being a stay-at-home mom. It was love at first touch! I, like so many others who pick up their first bar, was hooked. Polymer clay became my "fork in the road," the path that diverted me from my original intention to return to a television career when my kids started school. I never envisioned becoming a full-time artist, author, teacher, and designer, but the introduction of this amazing modeling compound was nothing short of miraculous.

The single most interesting phenomenon that I find when teaching is that many, if not most, of the people who are trying their hand at clay think it must be difficult to learn and master. Nothing could be further from the truth! I find that, given the proper instruction, resource information, and visual inspiration, most people can produce professional-quality and even saleable results immediately or with a little practice and experience.

Polymer clay's tactile appeal is only one of its many attributes and, by far, one of the most important. People are tactile and dimensional creatures by nature. We interpret what we feel, see, and think in a dimensional fashion. Don't believe me?

Close your eyes and picture an apple. Was your mental image a flat picture or an image with curves and dimensional perspective in your mind's eye? If you stop to think about it, you'll realize that you can easily take a 360-degree mental

tour of whatever it is you imagine as a picture. It's this ability that enables people to develop a high degree of skill with clay in a short amount of time. We are not two-dimensional creatures, and thus we are tactile by nature.

Polymer clay is the ideal art form, as it can be used by nearly everyone from children and hobbyists to fine artists. It can be manipulated into nearly every shape, texture, and consistency imaginable. Its flexibility as a mixed-media medium is nearly limitless. Polymer clay is truly the chameleon of the art world with its ability to be transformed into convincing versions of nearly any material you can think of—metal, porcelain, precious stones, glass, and more.

Within this book, you'll find techniques and applications both old and new. Some of these are discoveries I've made in my work over the years. Others are the brainchildren of well-known and not-so-well-known clay artists and enthusiasts. Many of these techniques and concepts have gone on to become universal in the clay world, such as the "Skinner Blend" method for creating color gradients, developed by Judith Skinner.

In the effort to maintain an ethical ideal in regard to the contents of this book, I have done my best to credit the originator of techniques whenever possible and to the best of my knowledge. The serendipity of near-simultaneous discovery over the years of same or similar concepts should be taken into account whenever the issue of artistic credit is involved. I consider this the positive proof of our creative ingenuity and imagination.

If you are new to clay and feel even the slightest hint of intimidation, I say feel the fear and clay it anyway! It's not as hard as you might think. If you have already discovered the joy of clay, I hope that you find a wealth of new ideas, techniques, tips, and inspiration within. The benefits of working with clay are many. "Claying around" can offer relaxation, spiritual connectivity, both physical and mental therapy benefits, and simply the satisfaction that comes from working with your hands. For some, it can even be the road to professional and monetary reward. Regardless of your motivation for picking up this book or the benefits you derive, I wish you the best of luck with all of your creative endeavors, and may every day be filled with clay!

Creatively yours,

Lisa Pavelka

I welcome your questions and comments. Please e-mail me at lisapavelka@cox.net.

CHAPTER ONE

Polymer Clay Essentials

YOU MAY BE WONDERING, "What, exactly, is polymer clay?" As opposed to earthenware clay, polymer clay is a manufactured modeling compound that remains soft until heated in an oven. Without getting too technical, polymer clay is a combination of polyvinyl chloride (PVC), plasticizer, and pigments. It bakes at low temperatures, typically between 230°F and 275°F. This allows you to bake it with a large number of materials that don't burn or melt at these low temperatures, like paper.

I have always maintained that polymer clay is the most versatile and forgiving medium on the planet. It is probably the most diverse; its fans and enthusiasts include children, hobbyists, model makers, jewelry makers, doll artists, professional crafters, and fine artists. It can be used for household repairs, like filling cracks in tile. It can even be drilled, carved, painted, sanded, polished, riveted, hinged, coiled . . . the list goes on and on.

A Brief History of the Medium

German doll artist "Fifi" Kruse Rehbinder developed a moldable material to use in the making of her doll heads in the 1930s. The compound was initially called "Fifi Mosaik." After the sale of the formula to German company Eberhard Faber in the 1960s, the company condensed the beginning of both names to rebrand the product FIMO®.

The next major product introduction to the clay world occurred in the 1960s, when Zenith Products Company, in Illinois, began selling a coating made for industrial use and as a modeling compound for hobby and crafting purposes. This was the very first Sculpey® product.

Polymer clay continues to undergo frequent changes and improvements. This is a tremendous plus for clay users everywhere. Improvements and additions to formula, strength, colors, durability, and safety are always under way.

Even though polymer clay has always been certified as nontoxic and, by all reports, safely used since its introduction, the manufacturers listed on pages 216–217 have removed phthalates, plasticizers common in use since the 1930s, from their clays as a safety precaution after the European Parliament banned these chemical compounds from toy manufacture in 2005. In 2009, the United States also banned phthalates from certain products. Fortunately, all of the major clay brands have complied with the European ban already in effect.

Types of Polymer Clay

There are several clay options available through craft stores and Internet resources, each with different benefits and limitations in regard to workability, strength, flexibility, firmness, working time, and a variety of other elements. Clay properties are discussed below under the individual clay brands.

The best determining factor for deciding which clay to work with is personal experience. The following is offered as a brief explanation of the most commonly available clays at the time of publication.

Most clay is sold in small bricks, typically weighing 2 oz. or more. The new Pardo clay by Viva Décor is sold in balls from packages of six balls (1.2 oz.) to larger jars of 2.65 oz. Some of these clays are also available in bulk-size bricks that range in size from 12 oz. to 16 oz. The best sources for the larger bricks of clay are catalogs and Internet sites. Many brands also offer color samplers in 1-oz. bars.

Generally speaking, all clays have an indefinite shelf life if properly stored. However, the amount of time clay remains in the conditioned state depends on the firmness of the clay.

There are more than a few brands of polymer clay that are designed for bulk or sculpting use (and come in only one color). For example, one bulk package that is a skin-tone base for doll sculpting is Polyform Super Sculpey®. (These will not be reviewed in the interest of simplicity.)

One great thing about working with clay is that, for the most part, it is not an expensive medium. While price fluctuations continue to occur within the retail market, the current cost of a small block or container ranges from two to three dollars. It follows that buying larger bulk bricks is usually less expensive.

The following is a breakdown of the most common polymer clay types.

CERNIT®

This clay is a favorite of doll makers because of the range of flesh-tone colors available and lifelike skin-tone translucency after baking. It can be somewhat difficult to condition, but it bakes very firm and strong with a good degree of flexibility. It's available in more than 60 colors.

FIMO CLASSIC

Originally only referred to as FIMO, FIMO Classic is the oldest and most widely recognized of the polymer clays due to its history. This clay is a favorite among fine artists and caners. It is one of the strongest and most resilient clays after baking, offering an excellent degree of flexibility. FIMO Classic bakes with a matte finish and is available in 24 colors.

FIMO SOFT

This is one of the easier clays to condition. A few seconds of kneading right out of the package is usually sufficient. FIMO Soft also offers the least amount of resistance or "blade drag" when slicing, even when very soft and warm. It has good strength and flexibility after bak-

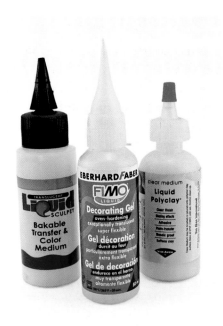

ing. It also offers one of the longest "open times" for working the clay as well as superior shelf life for millefiori canes | see MILLEFIORI CANING, chapter 4, page 44 |. It bakes with a matte finish and is available in more than 50 colors.

KATO POLYCLAY™

This clay is one of the newest brands, introduced earlier in this century. It can be stiff out of the package and take longer to condition, but it offers excellent strength and flexibility after baking. It bakes with a slight sheen and is available in 17 colors.

PARDO

This is the newest clay. It offers easy conditioning, superior strength, and re-usable packaging. It comes in over 70 colors.

PRĒMO! SCULPEY®

This clay offers a medium-soft consistency and bakes with excellent strength and flexibility while still being easy to condition. It is known for being stickier than other brands, which can be an advantage when, for example, you are doing the Sutton Slice and a limitation when you are rolling out long strips of clay such as with Skinner Blended bulls' eyes. It bakes with a slight sheen finish and is available in more than 30 colors.

SCULPEY III®

One of the first clays to be introduced in individual colors, this clay is very soft and easy to condition and offers good open time. It bakes firm with a matte finish, but it is not flexible and tends to be brittle after baking. This clay is best suited for projects with density and bulk, and it is available in more than 40 colors.

STUDIO™ BY SCULPEY

Softer than its sister clay, Prēmo! Sculpey, this clay offers easy conditioning. The feel is lighter and less dense than other clays, and it bakes with a matte finish. Its strength and flexibility are good, and it's available in more than 30 colors.

Liquid Clay

Liquid clay was first introduced in the 1990s. It remains an innovative addition to the polymer clay world and offers infinite possibilities. It can be used as a primary medium, especially when colored with oil-based paint, alcohol inks, or powdered pigments.

When adding color, mix only a drop or two at a time until the desired color is achieved. Try mixing some batches of colored liquid clay and store in small plastic bottles. Another handy way to prepare colored liquid clay is to fill empty paint pot strips, which are available at most craft stores.

Here are a few of the other applications for liquid clay:

- It can be used as an adhesive to bond clay layers together.

- You can use it to make image transfers, | see IMAGE TRANSFERS, chapter 5, page 62 |.

- You can add inclusions such as mica powder, glitter, and fibers to create specialty and stonelike effects.

- It makes an excellent sealer for foils, leafing, and transfers.

- It can even be used as a paper laminate.

Because the clay is liquid, you don't need to worry about having an uneven surface after you apply it. On the other hand, when using it as a sealer, be careful not to apply it too thickly, or the result will be a milky or cloudy surface. Sanding and buffing can be done after baking to polish and increase the clarity of thicker layers of polymer clay. Adding shine can also be achieved by adding glosses or glazes to cured layers of liquid clay.

APPLYING LIQUID CLAY

Liquid clay can be poured directly from the bottle or can be applied with a toothpick for detailed applications, with a fingertip, or by brush. (A high-quality hair or synthetic brush is recommended. Inferior brushes may lose bristles during application.) Once a brush has been used for liquid clay, it must remain dedicated to that clay use, as you will not be able to clean out all of the material.

Care for these brushes by wiping all the excess clay out of the bristles with a paper towel. Always stroke the towel in the direction of the bristles, away from the handle. Cover brushes with a small plastic bag with the handle facing down when stored. This will prevent dust and debris from contaminating the brush when not in use. Clean up liquid clay with baby wipes or alcohol.

Over time, the liquid clay may begin to thicken and firm up. To recondition a liquid-clay brush, work a few drops of fresh medium into the bristles to soften the old buildup. Drag the tip of a toothpick through the bristles to loosen and remove the excess clay. Wipe with a paper towel and repeat as needed until the brush is clean.

An alternative method for curing liquid clay is to use a heat gun designed for embossing powders. You can visibly see when the clay has set. The sheen will disappear, marking a change in the surface tension, indicating the clay has cured.

Liquid clay is commonly available in 2-oz. bottles, but indicated (*) brands below also come in 8-oz. sizes.

FIMO LIQUID DECORATING GEL

This is the clearest of the liquid clays and also has the lowest viscosity (thickness). It is highly flexible after baking. Extremely thin layers provide a matte finish, and thicker layers create a satiny gloss finish.

*KATO LIQUID POLYCLAY™

This liquid clay offers the second greatest clarity and has a medium thickness. It cures with the most flexibility and results in a satiny gloss finish in thick or thin applications.

*TRANSLUCENT LIQUID SCULPEY

This is the thickest of all liquid clays and has the least amount of clarity when cured. It can be thinned with Sculpey Diluent, which can also help when conditioning stiff clay. It cures hard and firm with a matte finish.

heat gun safety tips

Heat guns emit temperatures in excess of those recommended, making it possible to scorch or burn your clay.

First, make sure the work area is clean of uncured clay and any other flammable materials before working with a heat gun.

Tie your hair back and make sure any loose clothing is secured. Hold the gun about 3 in. to 5 in. away from the clay, moving it continuously in circles until the clay is cured.

The tip of the gun will be very hot after using. Allow it to cool before storing, about 10 to 15 minutes.

Safety First

In classes, I usually offer two rules for working with polymer clay: "Don't eat it and don't burn it," followed by, "Everything else is just a suggestion!" While that is basically true, there are some specific safety issues that must be shared.

1 Never leave uncured clay on a painted, varnished, or lacquered surface. Baked clay is inert and cannot harm furniture.

2 Polymer clay is rated as nontoxic, but it is not recommended for food use. Kitchen tools used for working with clay should remain craft or clay dedicated.

note

Shine occurs when baking on smooth surfaces like tile, but it can be removed with a light sanding with 1,000-grit or higher sandpaper.

note

Paper can curl when baking. For very thin pieces of clay, it can be helpful to bake directly on the tile or weight down the clay with a book after baking, to flatten.

You can't eat or drink from polymer clay, so don't even think about using anything made of clay for utensils or dishware. On the other hand, using it to embellish handles or the bases of stemware that don't come into contact with anything edible is fine.

3 Always clean hands thoroughly before handling food after working with clay. Use a pumice-based, waterless hand cleaner (available in the automotive section of many stores) or hand sanitizer to dissolve the clay residue. Follow with soap and water.

4 Never leave baking clay unattended! If clay appears to be smoking or burning, turn off the oven, remove the clay, and place it outdoors until cool. Ventilate the room.

5 Wear protective eyewear and use a dust mask or dust cabinet when carving, dry sanding, machine buffing, or drilling clay.

Work Surfaces

A smooth ceramic tile is the best work and baking surface. It's inexpensive and almost impervious to scratching, and it can go directly from your worktable into the oven. You may want several for your workstation.

Parchment-type deli paper (also known as patty paper) is ideal when you do not want your clay to stick to the work surface. (You'll soon discover when you want your clay to stick to the tile and when you don't.) Working with paper allows you to remove worked clay from your tile without stretching or distorting it.

You can find this type of paper in bulk at grocery warehouses and restaurant supply stores. You can even bake on it to prevent shiny spots from forming on the underside of your clay.

Clay Conditioning and Handling

All polymer clays must be conditioned, no matter how soft. Conditioning is the redistribution of all the ingredients that may have settled during storage. Failure to condition may lessen the finished strength of your baked clay. Clay is adequately conditioned when you can fold it without cracking.

Softer clays like FIMO Soft, Pardo, and Sculpey III can usually be conditioned straight out of the package by hand kneading for a minute or two. Slicing sheets from the block and repeatedly rolling them through a pasta machine several times is also a great way to condition your clay.

Leaching is a process by which plasticizer is removed from the clay. Although this technique will make the clay firmer to work with, it should be noted that it can also lessen the finished strength of the piece.

To begin the leaching process, sandwich thin slices of clay between several layers of copy paper. Place this on your work tile and set a phone book on top. How firm you want your clay to be is up to you, so this will require some monitoring on your part. A few hours may be enough, or you may need to allow the clay to rest a day or two, replacing the paper each time you see it is saturated through (this will appear as a grease stain). Remember that leaving unbaked clay on painted, varnished, or lacquered surfaces can damage their finish.

Firmer clays are naturally harder to condition and can sometimes be crumbly. Conditioning with a pasta machine should only be done after getting the clay warm and partially conditioned by hand.

Clay is very responsive to the heat of your hands. Some brands of clay will continue to get softer and softer in consistency when being handled.

Always begin working with the lightest colors of clay first whenever possible. Clay is like a magnet. It will pick up anything on your hands or work surface. Baby wipes—regular or alcohol-free—are ideal for cleaning your hands between colors of clay. A word of caution about generic brands of wipes: These can be very fibrous and may contaminate your clay with tiny particles of lint.

Baking

Polymer clay can be cured in ovens, including conventional, toaster, and convection types. Never use a microwave oven! And even though thousands of people have baked their clay in their food ovens for decades without incident, it's best to err on the side of caution and use a dedicated clay oven. If this isn't possible, you can create a "baking chamber" to use in your home oven. This is simply a roasting pan or large lidded pot that you dedicate for clay baking. If the piece is too tall for the lid to fit, tightly wrap a tent of aluminum foil over the baking pan.

Always follow the manufacturer's instructions for baking time and temperature. Preheat the oven and *always* use an oven thermometer to check for accuracy. I can't stress this enough.

Inexpensive tabletop ovens and toaster ovens have a tendency to fluctuate in temperature, especially if moved. Spikes in household electrical current can also cause heat surges. Be sure to always calibrate the oven by preheating and checking its temperature with an oven thermometer before baking clay.

Technically speaking, you cannot overbake your clay if you follow the above rules and the clay is at least 2 in. to 3 in. away from the heating elements and sidewalls.

The general rule of thumb for baking time is 20 minutes for every ¼ in. of thickness. Determine the baking time based on the thickest part of your piece.

conditioning tips

- Start by cutting the clay block into thin slices (about $1/8$ in. thick) with a clay blade. Working one slice at a time, firmly roll over the clay using an acrylic roller on your work tile. Fold the clay in half and repeat this step several times until the clay begins to soften. You should now be able to finish conditioning with a pasta machine or by kneading.

- Always roll clay through a pasta machine with the fold side down to prevent air bubbles from forming.

- Another option is to mix in small amounts of translucent clay. Adding too much can reduce color saturation or opacity.

- Add a few drops of liquid clay and knead thoroughly. If more is needed, add it sparingly and knead it into the clay before adding more, or a goopy mess may result!

- Place wrapped blocks on a zippered food bag containing $1/2$ cup of rice or barley that has been microwaved for no more than 30 to 45 seconds (this will stay warm for up to an hour). Unwrapped clay can be set on the bag (with a cloth in between) to prevent overheating of your clay. Placing the clay directly on a bag that is too hot may cause the clay to cure prematurely. Some people have even been known to sit on their unwrapped bars or put them in their pockets to aid in conditioning. Never put polymer clay in a microwave to soften or cure!

Some clay will darken in color somewhat when baking, even at the recommended temperature.

This applies to all brands of clay unless otherwise noted on the package.

Insufficient baking time or baking temperature will result in weak, brittle pieces. It's okay to double and even triple baking time to ensure optimal strength as long as you follow the rules above. You may find that in a classroom situation, your work may not have been exposed to correct times or temperatures. When in doubt, rebake the piece at home as if it was uncured.

When creating complex projects with multiple components, it can be helpful to bake the piece for 5 minutes to set the clay. Once cool, the clay will feel fully cured, but don't be fooled. This is "temporary heat setting," and it allows for the continued handling of clay without the risk of damage as you continue to add to the piece. The final baking should be timed as if the piece is going into the oven for the very first time.

Calculate your baking time according to the rule of 20 minutes for every ¼ in.

Let clay cool completely before handling. All clays will be slightly soft while warm and are typically fragile in this state. This can be advantageous if the clay has bubbled or warped during baking. Apply gentle pressure or weight to these areas while still warm using an oven mitt or the flat side of a rubber tex-ture stamp. Do not directly touch the clay straight out of the oven, as it may be hot enough to burn skin. To reshape the clay as desired, hold it flat or around a shape until cool. Use care when doing this. Drastically attempting to alter a shape while warm can cause breakage.

Clay Storage

Polymer clay doesn't require fancy or expensive storage. The main thing to do is to keep it out of heat and direct sunlight. Air won't dry out clay, as it contains no water. If your clay is being left out for extended times, cover it to prevent the accumulation of dust and debris—that is, unless you like the look of pet hair as an inclusion! And keep in mind that, in general, older clay may be much harder to condition.

Some methods for storing polymer clay are not recommended. Cured clay is inert, but uncured clay can react to certain types of plastic or other containers. Storing clay in paper, cardboard, or wood containers or drawers can draw plasticizer out of the clay, staining the container and weakening the finished quality of the clay.

Hard, inflexible plastic containers that are crystal clear or opaque are *not* suitable for storing uncured clay. These are made from solvent-based plastics that will react by melting when in contact with uncured clay. Here's what to look for in a plastic container that is appropriate for storing clay:

The material should be similar to food and household storage tubs—it should be somewhat flexible and won't fracture if broken. This type of plastic is soft and is either translucent or colored.

Those just starting to work with clay may wish to use inexpensive zippered food bags for storage. For a more systematic approach to clay storage, there are lots of great plastic containers available, including some with divided compartments and trays. These are wonderful for organizing clay by color or brand. It also makes transporting clay to classes and guild meetings a breeze.

Many fishing tackle boxes are made from the correct type of plastic and are great for home organization, especially if you do not have a dedicated workspace. Plano Molding Company sells a huge number of reasonably priced tackle boxes and modular cases for fishing that are very handy. They also have introduced their Creative Options™ craft line of storage containers that are clay compatible. The largest selections for storage are usually found in sporting goods and craft stores, but also look for them at dollar and discount department stores.

You'll occasionally find yourself with scraps and blended sheets you wish to keep for later use. Cut the outer edge of a plastic page cover (available at office supply stores) two-thirds of the way down. Place the clay inside these sheets and store in a three-ring binder.

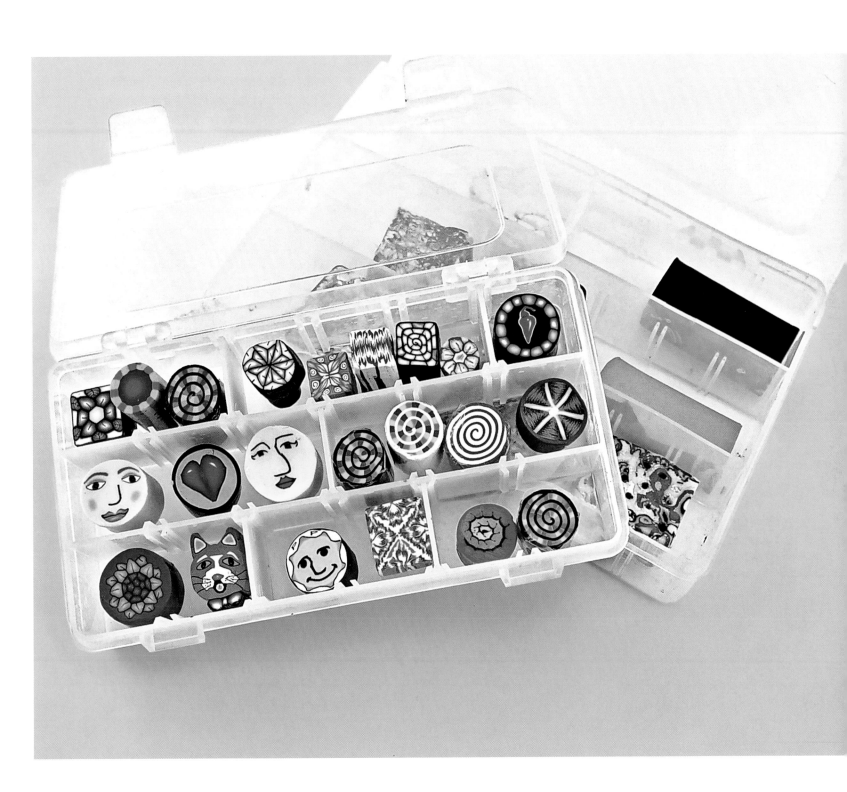

STORING MILLEFIORI

Storing millefiori canes for periods of time from weeks to years can result in the uncured clay becoming brittle. Reconditioning to render canes usable again is required in most instances. Warming a cane in your hand and/or reducing the size of the cane following recommended reduction techniques | see MILLEFIORI CANING, chapter 4, page 44 | can make a cane pliable once again for slicing and rolling. I avoid this problem by caning with softer clays. These canes seldom, if ever, require reconditioning before slicing, even after prolonged storage. If a cane slice crumbles when sliced or cracks when rolling to a thinner dimension, the cane must be reconditioned by one of the methods above.

Proper storage can ensure that you have years and years of workability with your uncured clays.

Color Basics

There are hundreds of resources devoted to color theory. It is often an intimidating concept to many. Common definitions regarding color appear below, while some additional terms, such as *value, tone,* and *shade,* are covered in the glossary section of the book | see GLOSSARY, page 211 |. The goal of this section is to offer helpful advice for working with color while taking some of the uncertainty out of the process.

- Primary colors are red, yellow, and blue. These colors are the basis for all the other colors seen on a standard color wheel. By mixing two primaries together, a secondary color is created.

- Secondary colors are orange (the mixture of yellow and red), green (the mixture of blue and yellow), and purple (the mixture of red and blue). On the color wheel, they're located in between the primary colors.

- Tertiary colors are in-between colors that occur when mixing one primary with one secondary color, such as blue-green.

- Complementary colors are colors that appear directly across from each other on the color wheel. The name is misleading. Complementary colors often don't show well when mixed together. These are colors that offer the highest contrast when used together.

- Analogous colors are those that appear right next to one another on a color wheel. They often match well when used together but can lack contrast.

Before the introduction of individually colored clays, users had to resort to painting or tinting the medium. How wonderful that polymer clay comes in a large array of colors and effects (including translucent and mica-based metallic)!

Just as with paint, clay can be mixed together until blended to create exciting new colors and shades that aren't available for purchase.

There are several considerations to make when selecting clay colors for a project. If you are looking for impact, consider working with high-contrast or complementary colors. If your aim is subtlety, turn to analogous colors and softer shades.

A wonderful resource is *The Color Index* book series by Jim Krause. These books contain thousands of two-, three-, and four-color combination samples. Also illustrated are side-by-side comparisons of colors in an illustrative application. It can be eye-opening to see the dramatic difference when certain color combinations play off one another in a graphic field as opposed to seeing them side by side.

Another means of getting color inspiration is to study food packaging. The food industry is highly competitive. Huge sums of money are spent in researching the types of colors and combinations that will attract attention. Consider cereal packaging. In grocery store aisles, the choices are staggering. Careful examination may surprise you when you stop and think about the colors that are combined.

In recent years, we've begun to see a huge departure from the color "rules," especially in fashion. Many industries have rethought the color rules many of us were taught as children, such as never mix green and orange or pink and brown.

Don't be afraid to experiment and take risks with color. Like some of you reading this, I used to be intimidated by which colors to use together. I now find that many of my favorite color combinations are those I would have never previously considered. Even though a case can be made for subtlety, the combined use of harmonious colors can result in loss of definition, sometimes to the point where they are indistinguishable from one another. This is especially true when creating millefiori canes.

Color Recipes

Here's an easy way to make consistent custom color combinations, time after time, along with a quick and convenient reference chip chart.

Use clay or cookie cutters of any shape. Use the largest setting of your pasta machine to prepare clay for cutting. Punch out the desired clay colors mixed together by hand or through the largest setting of the pasta machine until blended.

Creating a desired color may require cutting fractional pieces of one or more colors being blended. This is especially true when custom blending to make a color match.

Keep a notepad handy for writing down amounts of color used. During formulation, you may make several adjustments to colors being blended. Once the desired color is achieved, you can break down the ratios to reflect a simpler formula.

Here's an example of a recipe created to make a custom color of ecru needed to match some fabric: I started with 2 parts white to ½ part brown to ¼ part yellow. What I ended up with when I was satisfied with the colors was 12 parts white to 6 parts brown to 4½ parts yellow as shown in the top left photo. The formula was simplified by dividing fractionally into the following ratio: 4 parts white to 2 parts brown to 1½ parts yellow.

Once you have a formula, make a chip chart, as shown in the photo at bottom left. These are great reference tools

to use for recreating custom colors at a glance. Take some of the blended clay and roll it through the third-largest setting of the pasta machine. Cut out a disk with a small (1-in.) circle or oval cutter.

Punch a smaller hole near the top with a ⅛-in. circle cutter or coffee straw. Use small rubber or metal stamps to mark the clay ratio formula, using abbreviations.

Be sure to use two to three letters to distinguish colors that start with the same letter. Bake the chip and string it on a cord or ball chain.

Since clay colors vary from brand to brand, it's a good idea to write which clay was used on the back of the chip with a permanent marker. Chip charts are also great to make for clay mixed with inclusions (see the top middle photo on page 147).

Finishing

In some cases, the natural baked finish of the clay will be just what you're looking for. Or you may want to alter its natural baked finish. For this, there are several options.

Clay can be given a matte finish from coarse to smooth by sanding with assorted grits of automotive- or lapidary-grade finishing papers. Polishing or adding a gloss or glaze is another method of adding shine. This section is devoted to hand-finishing clay for the purpose of achieving finishes from a satin look to a high-gloss shine.

Polishing is really a matter of smoothing a surface through several steps of

scratching with finer and finer abrasives. Buffing is actually a continuation of this process to bring out the optimal shine and smoothness of a polished piece.

This method is especially good for round or cylindrical objects that don't always take glazes. Applying a glossing agent to pen barrels, beads, and cabochons can be tricky if the thickness and drying time of the product allows it to flow and drip uncontrollably.

Begin by wet-sanding baked clay using 400- or 600-grit wet-dry sandpaper (depending on how smooth the clay is to start with). The papers should be automotive or lapidary grade. The grits of household-brand sandpapers can be much coarser, regardless of the number indicated. I recommend 3M® papers for automotive or lapidary application.

Sand in a basin filled with water or wear a dust mask. Wet-sanding is preferred. It not only keeps airborne dust

from entering your lungs, but it helps speed up the sanding process and allows the paper to last longer.

Each person develops his or her own sanding method depending on what's comfortable, but I like to cut my paper into small squares so it's easier to handle. Then I rotate the area being sanded often to prevent flat spots from forming.

Once the piece is as smooth as it can get with one paper, rinse the clay and move on to the next higher grit. You'll see that the grit becomes worn off as you work. Discard it when you've used all the visible surface area. Continue working through 800-, 1,000-, 1,500-, and 2,000-grit sandpaper if desired. Higher grits are available, but not necessarily worth working with if sanding is well done.

At this stage, you may be happy with the appearance and feel of the piece. Buffing will provide a higher shine. Vigorous buffing with a piece of old blue-jean denim is the most economical method. An even higher shine can be achieved by using a bench grinder or jeweler's buffing wheel.

BUFFING WITH A MUSLIN JEWELER'S WHEEL

Use a non-synthetic muslin wheel with no outwardly spiraling stitching. Stitching that radiates through the muslin layers from the center of the wheel actually makes the wheel more abrasive. If you can only find a wheel with stitching, cut and remove the stitching up to the leather or metal grommet that holds the wheel together.

Work in an area without breakable objects. It's important to wear a dust mask and protective eyewear at all times when buffing. You may notice the wheel emits a lot of lint and dust when new.

Even though this subsides over time, it will always release airborne particles. Replace the wheel when only a 1½-in. radius of muslin remains.

Turn the wheel on at full speed. Barely, barely, barely touch the clay to the wheel's surface while buffing. Center the area being buffed in the middle to top portion of the wheel facing you. With flat objects, do not angle the corners and edges into the muslin. This can cause the object to be pulled from your hand (and become a flying projectile). Always maintain firm control of the clay as you buff. Do not allow it to be pulled down and under the wheel. Make sure all loose hair and clothing is pulled back away from the area where you are working.

Pressing clay too firmly against the wheel will actually sand the clay and cause flat spots, even with a very soft muslin wheel. You'll know if you're applying too much pressure because the clay will become more and more matte in appearance instead of shiny. As with sanding, move the clay continually for best results.

This process may sound intimidating, but it's actually quite easy with just a little practice and care. The results are well worth it. Sanding and polishing polymer clay can be very fatiguing to the hands. Be sure to rest them often.

CHAPTER TWO

Tools and Accessories

ANY ARTIST WILL TELL YOU that the best and most important tools are your own hands. But what creative person doesn't love tools?

A surprising number of clay techniques and projects can be completed with only a few essential tools: a clay blade, a craft knife, and a pasta machine. With the hundreds (if not thousands) of tool and accessory options available today, it's hard not to become a tool junkie.

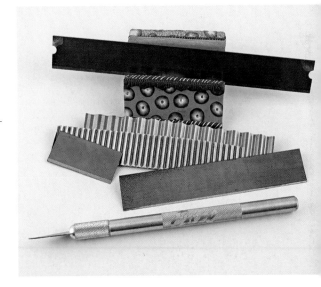

It would be impossible to list everything suited for polymer clay work in this book, so this section is devoted to an overview of the primary resources available. Some of the tools and products listed in this chapter will be revisited later in greater detail.

You may find that some of your favorite tools are those you repurpose from your kitchen or garage, or those you make yourself. Keep your eyes open in hardware, dollar, and discount specialty stores for unique tools, textures, and products that will allow you to broaden the range of your creations. Remember that tools designed for food need to remain dedicated to artistic use once used with polymer clay or other artistic mediums.

Tools

The tools used to work with polymer clay are generally not expensive or even that sophisticated, but having the essential ones is important.

BLADES AND KNIVES

It's critical to keep in mind that any blade is extremely sharp. The cutting edge can be recognized by the beveled angle found along the side. It's best to mark the corners of the dull side with some brightly colored nail polish or a permanent marker to distinguish between the two. Never let anyone under the age of 18 handle one without supervision.

Both straight and wavy blades were originally developed for medical and food

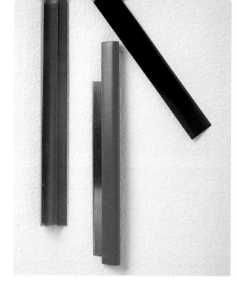

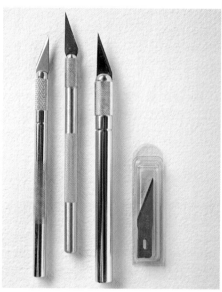

tips

• Keep an old clay blade reserved specifically for scraping dried residue off blades.

• Safely dispose of old blades by baking them between two thick layers of scrap clay before placing in the trash.

• Make a safety stand or trough to keep your blade safely out of the way and positioned for easy pickup. This is yet another way to use scrap clay.

    Form a 3-in.- to 4-in.-long U-shaped trough that's flat on the bottom and bake. Cover it with decorative clay and rebake.

tip

Gently pulling the blade by the upper corners when slicing will prevent bowing and provide cleaner, more even slices.

uses. Soon after clay users began to work with them, the manufacturers of arts and crafts supplies began offering straight and specialty blades. There are now a variety of blades with different lengths, degrees of flexibility, and specialty shapes that cut clay in patterns.

Other blades, such as wallpaper scrapers and straight-edge razors, are not suited for clay work. They are typically too thick or may feature a dimensional safety edge that makes cutting thin, precise slices difficult.

Proper blade handling is also important. When cutting, blades should always be held by the corners. Do not press your fingers down across the top edge. Even though the edge is dull, application of heavy pressure can cut skin in some cases.

When working with a new blade, clean and condition it first with 800- or 1,000-grit automotive- or lapidary-grade sandpaper. This will remove the coating applied to prevent rust from forming during shipping and shelving.

To periodically clean and sharpen your blades, follow a few guidelines. Fold the sandpaper in half and sandwich it between a small piece of fabric or sponge, which acts as a safety buffer for your fingers. Slide the sandpaper down along the edge several times, leaving some space between the blade and the folded edge as a safety precaution. Be sure to do this along both sides of the blade to help remove buildup that can cause drag. Only use a baby wipe or alcohol to clean the blade to remove glue, liquid clay, or paint. Dry the blade immediately to prevent rust and corrosion.

A blade is no longer usable when the beveled edge measures less than 1 mm wide or notches begin to form along the bottom. Proper blade care can prolong its life for months and even years.

Craft knives with handles are invaluable for detailed cutting, piercing air bubbles, or picking up tiny elements. These knives have a screw collet that holds the blade securely in place. The #11 blade is considered the standard for these handles, but many options for different shapes and sizes can be found at hardware, craft, and hobby stores.

TRAVELING WITH TOOLS

Changes in airline travel since September 11, 2001, have greatly altered the way we must transport tools and creative supplies. It is possible to travel with most tools and supplies, but only in checked luggage. Here are some great tips to bear in mind:

• Due to screening and inspection policies (as of when this book was published) it's important to securely pack all tools and supplies in separate storage containers or boxes that are clearly marked with the contents.

• Attach a note that says, "Open with care, sharp art tools inside." If an inspector is injured by a tool when opening your luggage, he or she will be more likely to confiscate it.

- Only nonflammable art materials can be checked in your luggage. Polymer clay and liquid clay are fine to check in luggage. Note that security policies can change at any time. It's best to check with the airlines and the Transportation Security Administration (TSA) each time you fly to remain current on restrictions.

- Double-bag all liquids and powders. Cargo holds are not pressurized. This can cause containers to expand and possibly leak.

- Inspection officials or bag jostling can cause storage containers and boxes to open. Secure all containers with elastic headbands or small bungee cords.

Clay Forming

This section is devoted to the tools used for rolling, shaping, and sculpting polymer clay.

PASTA MACHINE

Many consider this to be the most essential item in a clayer's cadre of tools. Nearly all clay work can be done with an acrylic roller or brayer, but a pasta machine reduces the work and time needed to do numerous tasks and techniques. Only manual crank machines are suitable for clay, but electric motors are available for these machines (more about motors on page 26).

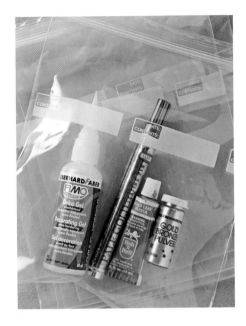

tips for the pasta machine

- The clamp that comes with the machine doesn't fit onto many tables and can break easily if too much pressure is applied when tightening. Consider instead using one or two large, deep C-clamps to attach your machine to the table.

- Forcing too much clay through any setting can result in permanent damage to your pasta machine over time. You will know if this has occurred when clay rolled out through the thinnest settings no longer comes off the rollers under the machine. This is an indication that the guide blades beneath may be bowed.

  Continual forcing of too much clay through any setting bends these blades. The resulting gap will prevent the blades from lifting the clay off the rollers.

  Before inserting clay through the largest setting, slice it from a block into thin sheets. If the clay crumbles when rolling, follow the *conditioning tips* found in chapter 1, page 13.

- Periodically turn the machine over to wipe away the buildup that accumulates on the guide blades. Follow by repeatedly rolling a large sheet of scrap clay through the machine to pick up any loosened bits that may otherwise contaminate your clay after cleaning the machine.

- It's possible to take apart most machines for cleaning, but it's not absolutely necessary. It can also be difficult or impossible to reassemble some machines.

  After years of taking my machine apart to clean it, I discovered a very simple trick that prevents "hitchhiking" bits of clay from contaminating the clay I'm rolling: Cover the clay you are rolling with a deli sheet. This protects the surface from possible color contamination. More information on taking apart pasta machines can be found at www.glassattic.com.

In recent years, there has been an introduction of pasta machines intended specifically for polymer clay. Makin's Clay® offered the first major innovation in a pasta machine designed specifically for clayers. Their machine features Teflon®-coated rollers, which reduce or eliminate clay contamination.

Pasta machines come in roller lengths between 5½ in. and 8 in. They come equipped with a removable handle and an attachment clamp. Machine settings typically vary from seven to nine thick-

tip

Don't have a pasta machine? Roll clay between two identically stacked piles of playing cards until the roller makes contact with each. This will allow you to create clay sheets of uniform thicknesses.

ness settings. The thickness setting is adjusted by pulling a spring-loaded dial that turns both clockwise and counterclockwise. Some machines list the number 1 as the largest or thickest setting. On other machines, the largest setting may be the number 7 or 9. Acquaint yourself with your machine to know which the largest setting is. Because of this difference between machines, all recommended thickness settings in this book will be listed as "the largest setting," "the second-largest setting," "the third-largest setting," and so on.

New machines with stainless steel rollers may leave black marks on white and light-colored clays. Regularly clean the rollers with a baby wipe or rubbing alcohol. Avoid getting moisture into the machine. Internal components can rust. Periodically tighten the screws on the bottom and sides of the machine.

MOTOR

This accessory is very helpful to those with physical limitations or anyone who does large amounts of clay work. However, motors are very noisy and can take some time to get used to. They are available through clay suppliers and on the Internet. Motors attach in the opening where the crank handle is normally placed. There are two running settings: continuous turning and a pulse mode, which runs the rollers only when depressed. A foot pedal increases the versatility of the motor, allowing on-and-off control with a push of the foot and variable speed control not available through the button controls. Foot pedals are available through jeweler's supply resources.

HAND ROLLER

An acrylic roller or brayer is a primary tool for clay work. Metal and PVC piping are alternative types of rollers. Whatever works best for you is the right tool.

Rollers can be used to smooth ripples that can sometimes be formed by a pasta machine. They can also be used to flatten, condition, shape, or reduce clay canes. A roller offers more control for the clayer over the process of stretching and thinning clay than one would have using a pasta machine, which only offers set thicknesses.

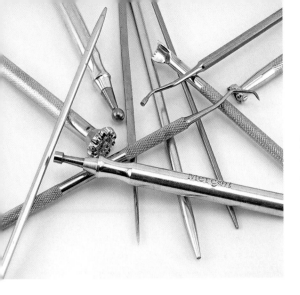

EXTRUDER

There are several types of extrusion devices made for modeling compounds. These come with assorted dies (disks) that control the size and shape of the clay that is extruded. Extruders force clay through the barrel using either a push plunger, a twist crank, or a squeeze trigger.

This tool is especially handy when long pieces of clay snakes or borders are needed. Extruders also offer more uniform shapes than snakes rolled by hand.

The softer and warmer the clay, the easier it is to extrude. Proper conditioning is essential to preparing clay for extrusion. Barrel sizes vary from small to large. Smaller extruders are best for most everyday uses. Large extruders are best suited to making components for the construction of large canes or home décor projects.

Extruders should be cleaned between color changes to prevent cross contamination.

HAND TOOLS

A needle tool is considered a staple tool for clay users, and there are myriad other hand tools to choose from. There are rubber-end tools for smoothing, blending, and shaping. They come in a variety of shapes, from chisel edges and blunt edges to pointed and rounded tips.

Ball-tip styluses in varying sizes are great for texturing clay. There is also an increasing number of hand tools designed expressly for texturing clays, including some with rolling, interchangeable texture wheels. Pouncing wheels for sewing also make a nice addition to any tool kit.

Leather stamping tools are ideal for clay. Since they are metal, they can stick to clay. Application of a release agent to clay beforehand can be helpful | see MOLDS, page 30, for more information |.

Metal knitting needles come in all types of sizes and diameters. These can be used to create texture, draw impressions, or even substitute for clay rollers.

Dental picks and wood-carving tools can be great fun to use. Consider nontraditional options like the open end of a

tip

Raise the bar on creative inspiration by creating your work with a piece of artwork in your hand! Consider covering your metal- and wood-handled tools with clay. It's also a great way to personalize tools in order to distinguish them from others in a class or group setting.

tips for cleaning extruders

Lay the clay log to be extruded over a piece of plastic food wrap. The plastic should be wide enough to roll around the clay one-and-a-half to two times. It should be about 1 in. longer than the length of the clay log. Align the clay on the plastic so it is parallel to one edge of the plastic's edge. Roll the wrap around the clay. Twist the extended end like a taffy wrapper.

Inset the clay into the barrel with the exposed end against the extruder opening. Once the clay has been extruded, take the device apart to remove the plastic wrap, leaving the barrel clean.

Here's another cleaning option for metal clay extruders only. Bake the barrel in the oven for 5 to 10 minutes at the same temperature recommended for the brand of clay used. When cool, loosen and remove the hardened clay with a bamboo skewer. Remember, this is only for extruders with metal barrels.

retractable ballpoint pen. Cake icing tips make great fingertip tools for texturing, cutting out small clay circles, and even setting crystals.

Consider making your own needle tools and styluses by embedding straight pins and quilting pins into handles made from scrap clay.

BEAD ROLLER

Making uniformly sized and shaped beads from clay used to be a challenge for many. That hasn't been the case since Sue and Gale Lee of Poly-Tools invented their amazing bead rollers. I've had the pleasure of watching their tools improve and expand since the 1990s. This line offers a large variety of roller shapes and sizes. Simple instructions make measuring, rolling, and piercing clay effortless. Their clay tools are in a class by themselves!

Adhesives

Wouldn't it be great if there were a single glue for every application? Unfortunately, different materials have different adhesion properties. It's important to use the right adhesive for the right application. This section addresses only three of the most applicable adhesives for polymer clay.

Without getting too technical, it's important to know some basic information. I've been known to tell my classes that when it comes to creativity, "More is more, and less is a bore!" Not so when working with glue. There is a common misperception that if a little glue will work, a lot of glue will work better. Make no mistake, when it comes to glue, less is more. All glues require oxygen to cure. Applying too much glue will typically result in some of it being visibly exposed. Not only is this unsightly, it has a tendency to discolor. Even worse, the glue between the surfaces being bonded may

never fully cure, causing the bond to fail, sooner if not later.

Even with permanent adhesive applications, vibration, shock, and wear and tear can take its toll. Most polymer clays are very durable after curing, but breakage even under the best of circumstances is a reality. However, when the proper adhesive is used correctly, the need to glue again should seldom, if ever, occur.

CYANOACRYLATE GLUE

This type of adhesive is commonly known as "super glue." It works best on porous materials. Uncured clays generally bond well wherever they make contact prior to baking, especially if pressure between the clays has been applied.

In some cases, you may have dimensional or textured clay surfaces or elements that cannot be pressed together with any pressure. In other cases, you may wish to add a little "adhesive insurance" just to be on the safe side. Either way, a high-temperature cyanoacrylate is the ideal method for bonding polymer clays.

The challenge using this glue is that it has very little working time, setting up in only seconds. Apply only small amounts at a time when working on larger surfaces or when positioning components, since the bond is almost instant.

Cyanoacrylate is not recommended when adding clay to glass unless the entire surface is covered with clay. The same is true when adding clay to single flat surfaces made from plated metals. If edges or multiple sides of plated metal surfaces are covered, high-temperature bonder will work just fine.

Gluing to aluminum and other porous surfaces is typically permanent. If the surface is very porous, like paper or wood, sealing first with a thin layer of liquid clay and baking is advised.

Over-the-counter super glues intended for household or cosmetic use are not recommended for use with polymer clay for three reasons:

- Unless indicated on the label, cyanoacrylate super glues (and nail glues) are not intended for heating. Doing so may pose a safety or health concern.

- Regular cyanoacrylate glues begin to disintegrate at 125°F, meaning a strong, lasting bond is not ensured. High-temperature clay bonder is not only safe to bake, but the resulting bond will be strong. High-temperature cyanoacrylate can also be used for household repairs and crafting applications.

- For projects that require multiple bakings, you'll find that uncured clay doesn't like to stick to baked clay. Only a small amount of bonder is needed to connect raw and baked clays together. Areas where there is no glue making contact will still fuse together during the baking process.

LISA PAVELKA POLY BONDER™ GLUE

This was the first cyanoacrylate glue specifically intended for baking with polymer clay up to 300°F. Its low-odor and no-fog formula is a product I worked to develop for polymer clay and crafting. Poly Bonder features a nonclog brush-on applicator bottle.

EPOXY

This type of adhesive is a two-part glue consisting of a resin and a hardener. Both parts must be mixed together in equal amounts. Epoxies come in setting times from 90 seconds to 5, 10, and 20 minutes or longer.

Epoxies are not designed for baking and should be used for applications after clay has cured. These are suggested for gluing clay components to glass and other nonporous surfaces.

Epoxy comes in tubes, double-barreled syringes, or bottles. The curing process begins immediately once mixing is started. Consider how much working time is needed for any given project. Even though most epoxies usually set very quickly, always allow the glue to cure for a full 24 hours before using your creation.

If only one side of a plated metal object is covered with clay, you may need to remove it after baking and reattach with epoxy. Carefully slide a clay blade between the two surfaces to loosen.

After baking, try to remove any nonporous embellishments (pearls, metal charms, and so on) and reattach with epoxy. However, if the item is resistant to removal after baking, don't force it. Another exception would be cases in which the item is secured with a clay embellishment or frame.

tips for using epoxy

- Mix epoxy on an index card or folded piece of aluminum foil using a toothpick. Discard excess glue after it has set.

- Rough up the surfaces of the two items being bonded together to get optimal adhesion. Use a needle tool or awl to make deep scratches in the back of the clay and the surface of the item you are attaching it to whenever possible.

LIQUID CLAY

Liquid clay can be used to bond two flat clay surfaces together. On vertical or curved surfaces, the liquid clay will remain slippery until heated for several minutes. This may result in the clay sliding away from its original position. High-temperature bonder is best for these types of applications. Liquid clay is also ideal for gluing clay to fabric.

Cutting and Shaping Tools

There is a nice variety of cutting and shaping tools available to clayers of all skill levels. These elements are straightforward and have evolved quite a bit for the polymer clay medium.

CUTTERS

There are many specific and nontraditional tool options for cutting clay into shapes. Some of the handiest and most interesting include cookie and canapé cutters. Cutting tools are not only handy for cutting specific sizes and shapes, but also for measuring out amounts of clay

tip

When using straws to make small circles or to create texture, cut them down to 1 in. in length so that if the clay sticks inside, it can be easily removed with a needle tool or toothpick.

for custom blending. There are even clay cutters that not only cut out clay shapes, but emboss designs into the surface.

Kemper Tools makes spring-loaded tools in assorted sizes and shapes for cutting out small clay forms. For an even larger number of cutting size options for small circles, try cake-decorating icing tips or drinking/coffee straws. These tools make wonderful polka-dot and decorative accents in clay work and can even be used as texture tools.

PUNCHES

Punches are not just for paper! Hand and decorative punches are perfect for die-cutting detailed clay shapes.

Clay should be baked first and rolled out very thin. Less flexible clays are not recommended for this application.

SCISSORS

Think outside of the box when it comes to cutting clay. Scissors are one of the most overlooked tools for clay work. You can use both straight-edge and decorative-edge scissors on uncured or baked clays. Cutting baked clay works best on very thin sheets.

Scissors can be especially handy when cutting off excess clay on wrap-around borders or in corners, since these areas can be difficult to access with a clay blade or craft knife.

MOLDS

These tools are wonderful for adding dimensional impact to your work. Molds can be a quick and easy way to create jewelry or to accent all types of creations. There are several manufacturers that make both rigid and flexible molds for clay. Some are specifically designed for clay but those used for other mediums can work just as well.

You can even make your own molds using scrap clay or self-vulcanizing silicone compound that mixes much like epoxy.

Make molds from figurines, buttons, seashells, findings, antique jewelry, or your own clay originals.

When using a mold made from polymer clay, the uncured clay must be removed prior to baking. Use of a release agent is recommended on plain clay. Applying clay foil, leafing, or mica powders to clay before molding acts as a release agent with decorative benefits.

I recommend an automotive protectant spray like STP® Son-of-a-Gun!® or Armor All® Protectant as a release agent. They will not affect the clay and are safe to handle.

Other options include dusting the mold with cornstarch. This will leave a residue that is easily washed away with water after baking. It will, however, affect a slight change in the surface texture of the clay. Water can also be used but it is a last resort since it beads and doesn't ensure good overall coverage.

- Use clay scraps that contain brown, black, or gray, as these colors, when mixed with more vibrant colors, will result in dull, muddy tones.

- Be sure to mix the clay completely, using plenty of scrap to ensure the mold isn't thin and brittle. If the clay is left marbled, it can be hard to visually determine if the mold has been properly filled.

- Whenever possible, extend the clay beyond the piece you are molding. This will leave a nice, clean edge, making it easy to trim excess clay away.

Silicone molds are flexible and don't require a release agent, although it's still best to use one. This will minimalize or prevent distortion when bending the mold to release the clay.

Another option for a clean release without loss of detail is to bake the clay directly in the silicone mold. This is safe to do. When the clay is cool, it should pop out nicely.

METAL STAMPINGS

Try working with vintage metal stampings, which can be found in bead stores and flea markets. These elements were designed for jewelry and architectural adornment but they lend themselves beautifully to clay molding. They are typically convex and feature finely detailed relief.

Backfill the stamping with conditioned clay and slice off the excess, leaving the backing flush with the edges of the metal.

INTAGLIOS

These are vintage glass components that work much the same way as stampings but are generally not as deep. Intaglios are incised (or negative) carvings. Historically, they were used for making seals for wax embossing. Later this technique was adapted for making jewelry and decorative adornments in glass and crystal, among other things.

Clay can be directly baked in stampings and intaglios. No release agent is necessary. After baking and cooling carefully, pry or pop out the clay using the tip of a craft knife. Strong, flexible brands of clay work best for this method since these molds are typically shallow and the clay will be thin.

tips

- Additional suggestions for decorating molded clay include applying mica powder to the raised areas after molding or antiquing with paint after baking.

- When working with face molds, roll the clay ball into a slight teardrop. Insert the pointed end into the nose cavity to ensure proper filling of this space.

- When working with automotive spray, apply a small amount to the clay rather than the mold (the same holds true when stamping clay). Spread over the entire surface with your fingers. This will ensure cleaner release.

Textures

While the subject of texture was touched upon in the Hand Tools section of this chapter, rubber stamps and plastic rubbing plates offer some of the most exciting products for adding texture and dimension to clay surfaces. Many of the techniques that appear in this book rely on the use of texture. Textures enhance both unadorned and treated clay surfaces, including those that have been foiled, painted, or powdered.

They can also be used to achieve some of the techniques found in this book, including Mokumé Gané (pronounced may-ku-may gone-ay), the Sutton Slice, and Mica Shift, to name a few.

A favorite texture tool of mine is very coarse sandpaper. Impressing fabrics or lace into clay is also a fantastic technique for texturing. You can even find interesting textures on the soles of shoes (clean, of course!).

Even the collet on most craft knives can be removed and used as a rolling texture tool, embossing the clay's surface with a fine, repeating diamond pattern.

Other suggestions include aluminum foil, leaves, buttons, and even embedded salt (in different coarsenesses), which can be dissolved with water after baking.

Open yourself up to the amazing array of textures all around you. Adding dimension to your work creates richness and depth (literally and figuratively). The best part is that if you're not happy with the end result, you can always roll the clay back out and start all over!

Inclusions and Surface Treatments

The products listed in this category are excellent for both surface applications and placement under thin layers of translucent clays (liquid and block varieties). Mixed use of these products will not only heighten the playfulness of clay creations, but they can also help to expand your own unique style.

CRYSTALS

Only genuine crystal should be baked with clay. Plastic or acrylic stones will melt. CRYSTALLIZED™–*Swarovski Elements* come in a huge number of sizes, styles, colors, and effects. They are all ideal components for embellishing polymer clay.

In order for a crystal to stay secure in clay, it must be pressed down into the clay until the clay rises up over and around the edges, forming a naturally occurring bezel, which locks the crystal in place. If a crystal falls out of clay after baking, it is an indication that it wasn't pressed deep enough. This is easily fixed by replacing the crystal using jewelry cement.

The most widely used crystals for clay are "flatbacks." These come as regular flatbacks (no adhesive), with Hotfix® (a patented heat-sensitive adhesive for textiles), and as chatons (pointed-back stones).

While a crystal that's properly secured needs no adhesive, it can be advantageous to work with the Hotfix variety since the heat of the oven activates the glue on the back. This allows for a more secure setting of the stone without the need to bury it as deeply. The higher a faceted stone sits in your clay, the better the light refraction and sparkle will be.

MICA POWDERS

FIMO Metallic Powders, Jacquard Pearl Ex, and Ranger Perfect Pearls are pigmented mica powders that can be used to enhance smooth, textured, and molded clay. Applied in heavier layers, they can mimic the look of metal.

Powders can be applied with a fingertip, a foam cosmetic applicator, or a brush. They can also be mixed into liquid clays and resins.

These powders come in a variety of colors. Stippling multiple hues onto clay with a fingertip results in a beautiful variegated effect. Pearl Ex and Perfect Pearls are also available in "interference" colors. These are opalescent colors that change in tone and shade when applied to various colors of clay.

FIMO Metallic Powders and Pearl Ex should be sealed after baking with brush-on polymer-clay-compatible lacquer or resin. This will prevent the powders from coming off from direct contact with skin and clothing. Perfect Pearls has a built-in resin that allows it to bond to the clay during baking. No sealing is required.

FIMO Metallic Powders are available individually. Pearl Ex and Perfect Pearls are available both individually and in sets. Pearl Ex is also available in larger bulk sizes.

EMBOSSING POWDERS

Also known as thermographic powders, these products are used by printing houses and rubber stampers to create raised impressions on paper. Embossing powders can be added to clay by hand-kneading in tiny pinches at a time. Mixing with the pasta machine is not recommended.

These powders come in all types of colors. They melt when baked in the clay. The effect is known as "blooming" and creates a speckled pattern that shows across the clay's surface. The more powder added, the more intense the speckling will be.

Many embossing powders are only encapsulated with color on the outside, but are white on the inside. The typical result is that the powder will bloom white, regardless of the exterior color. The only way to be sure what color you'll end up with is to test-bake a pinch in the desired color of clay.

GLITTER

This product has come full circle from the glitter we knew as children. There are more refined brands, colors, and effects available. Barbara Trombley's Art Glitter offers one of the largest varieties of glitter suitable for use with clay.

Some glitters burn while baking. While this isn't actually hazardous, the resulting effect is glitter that looks dull and flat. High-quality products like Trombley's glitter come in different sizes and grades, from microfine to larger flakes. These offer superior light refraction, metallic property, and shine. They are even available in custom color blends. Another benefit to these higher-quality glitters is that they do not

safety tip

Embossing powders are easily airborne, and inhalation should be avoided. Do not use in drafty rooms and keep tightly capped when not in use.

develop an annoying static charge, enabling them to be easily cleaned up from your work area.

Glitter should only be mixed into clay in small amounts (as with embossing powder). Adding more to intensify the effect should be done gradually. It can also be stirred into translucent and colored liquid clays.

PAINT

Acrylic and tempera paints work well on polymer clay. These can be used before or after baking clay to create different effects, like antiquing and crackle finishes. Applying paint dimensionally (in layers) like gesso is also a way to achieve distressed and vintage effects popular in the altered art and collage traditions.

Rub 'n Buff® from AMACO® is a pigmented wax that is ideal for use on baked clay. It is especially good for creating antiqued and patinated finishes. Disposable gloves are recommended for applying this product.

tip

It can be fun to mix embossing powder with glitter to get varied effects. FIMO Soft and Pardo clays offer several colors already embedded into the clay.

PATINA AGENTS

These are two-part products that contain fine particles of real metal. They can be used to give polymer clay the appearance of being rusted, or of patinated bronze or copper. One brand that works well on clay is Sophisticated Finishes, which can be found at most craft stores and on the Internet.

INKS

Rubber stamp pads are an excellent way to create several looks on the surface of clay. Both pigment- and dye-based inks become permanent when baked on clay. Stamps can be used to deliver ink in a dimensional embossed method or just to the surface, much like they would apply it to paper. Exciting introductions of specialty inkpads can further expand the creative possibilities of working with this medium. They include chalk and metallic finishes.

Alcohol inks can be blended into liquid clay. Unlike oil-based paint, which

will color liquid clay with opacity, these inks will tint the clay while retaining a translucent quality. Sponging or painting ink onto clay can also be used to create interesting backgrounds.

CLAY FOIL

Both clay foil and metal leaf add metallic properties to clay, but they are two very different products. Foil is mounted on a Mylar® backing. It is burnished onto uncured polymer and adheres through heated application, whereas metal leaf is directly applied to the clay.

This product is intended for clay but is also suitable for other creative applications with the use of tacky glues or double-sided adhesives. Clay foils come in a variety of metallic colors and patterns, such as rainbow and oil slick.

There is even a translucent oil slick that reveals the color of the clay to which it is applied. It can be layered with transfers and leafing.

Clay foil can be used to achieve faux dichroic and art glass effects, especially when sealed under layers of dimensional resin. Techniques for these and other applications can be found in the chapters that follow.

Foil will crackle when stretched, but not as dramatically as leaf does. The effect is a much softer look.

LEAF

This product comes in sheets of micro-thin metal. It is found in two varieties: the genuine precious metals and the much less expensive version known as

composite leaf. Most people cannot tell the difference between the real thing and composite leafing, but the difference in price is staggering. Composite leaf comes in the three most common metallic tones—gold, silver, and copper—as well as variegated metallics. It is also available in mixed color flakes. It is very delicate and fragile. Leaf tears and crackles very easily.

Leafed clay that is exposed to repeated handling should be sealed with a brush-on lacquer or resin to prevent the leaf from flaking off over time.

IMAGE TRANSFERS

While the subject of transfers is covered in later chapters, it's worth noting that there are transfers made especially for polymer clay use. These are also suitable for crossover application with mediums including wood, glass, paper, and a variety of other surfaces. They are just one of the options for adding pictorial embellishment to your clay work. These transfers are available in preprinted and customizable inkjet media and work the same as waterslide decals for model making.

ANGELINA® FIBERS

These are fine, fusible fibers with a metallic sheen. They come in many gorgeous colors and effects, including holographic and iridescent fibers. They are ironed into flat layers between parchment papers or Teflon craft sheets. A traditional iron set between medium and high heats will bond the fibers together in a few seconds.

tips

• Some foil colors may fade in higher baking temperatures. After applying foil, bake for 3 to 5 minutes and then seal with a thin fingertip application of liquid clay to prevent fading.

• If foil fades during baking or if deeper tones are desired, color over the foil with permanent markers to intensify the saturation.

• Try using some different colored permanent markers over contrasting foils to get a variegated effect.

Angelina fibers can add an interesting and glamorous look to clay surfaces, especially when sealed beneath layers of resin.

Finishes

There are a variety of options for giving baked clay work a glossy finish without the effort of polishing and buffing. It's important to use sealers and glosses that have been specified as clay compatible. Some glazes and glosses for household and craft applications contain solvents. Over time, solvent-based finishes will react with the clay, leaving them feeling permanently tacky. This is especially true of aerosol spray finishes.

FIMO Gloss Lacquer, Future® Floor Finish (available in most grocery store cleaning aisles), and Varathane® Diamond Water-Based Polyurethane all provide surface gloss without dimension. These types of products are best used on round and cylindrical clay forms such as pens, beads, and lentil shapes.

Keep in mind that applying these directly to cured clay without polishing first may result in a slightly mottled appearance. Polishing clay first | see POLYMER CLAY ESSENTIALS, chapter 1, page 19 | will smooth the surface and allow the sealer to dry with a high-gloss finish.

Future may be baked after application. Baking is not recommended with the other products listed above.

RESIN

There are several resins that work with baked clay. Many resins are epoxy based and require the mixing of two parts. Many of these types of resins will yellow over time. Typical drying time is several hours to one or more days.

In 2007, my own dimensional resin for clay and crafting was introduced. Lisa Pavelka Magic-Glos™ is a nontoxic, no-odor gloss that requires no mixing and dries in only minutes (5 to 15 minutes for most layers). It is cured by UV light (direct sunlight, a 6-watt or higher UV cure lamp, or a 40-watt or higher fluorescent black-light bulb). Even though heat doesn't have any effect in the curing process, the product can be baked at clay temperatures. This allows the user to continue adding clay embellishment to pieces already treated with cured gloss. Baking may also darken the gloss slightly but this isn't typically noticeable except with white and very light-colored clays and transfers.

Unlike nondimensional surface glazes, Magic-Glos is great for embedding accents and inclusions. It also gives foils and transfers the look of glass. Multiple layers can be added to create rounded or domed cabochon effects. It can also be matted (by sanding), drilled, or carved.

Keep in mind that other dimensional glazes are not always waterproof and may require sealing after drying to prevent them from becoming cloudy or tacky.

CHAPTER THREE

Skinner Blending

THOSE OF YOU NEW TO POLYMER CLAY may be thinking, "Polymer clay sure looks great in projects, but it must be difficult to get the results you see without being an expert." Nothing could be further from the truth. The beauty of this medium is that it has an extremely slight learning curve. The most difficult thing about clay is deciding to take the plunge. Because polymer clay is a technique-based medium, your skill improves exponentially with practice. The great news is that it takes most people very little practice to master the various techniques, and you can achieve professional-looking results rather quickly.

It has taken a long time for the polymer clay you buy today to evolve from its humble beginnings, and even though polymer clay has been around since the 1930s, its widespread popularity didn't begin to grow until it became available in colors besides white and beige tones. Not long after, visionaries like David Ford and Steven Forlano of City Zen Cane began experimenting with special visual effects that could be achieved through a gradient look.

The illusion of graduated color brought a sense of depth and dimension to the work of early pioneers in the medium. Artists and hobbyists could create a series of clay blends that, when layered, gave this gradient look. The more layers there were, the more realistic the effect.

TECHNIQUES

- Basic Skinner Blending
- Multiple-Color Skinner Blending
- Creating Surface Sheets
- Gradient Loaves
- Ribbons

My early experiments with this varied greatly depending on how much work I was willing to do in blending a color series. For more realistic-looking gradients, I created 100 shades from light to dark between two colors.

When I was interested in a less labor-intensive result, I might make only 10 to 30 shades between two colors. This could take hours or even days. The more shades that were layered, the more gradual the effect, but even with a higher number of shades, a somewhat striated appearance could still be seen.

Enter Judith Skinner, a brilliant clay artist who came up with a method for creating true gradient blends between two or more colors that took only minutes rather than hours or days. The term "Skinner Blend" is synonymous with color gradients made with polymer clay using two or more colors. This innovative method revolutionized clay work for thousands, not only allowing gradients to be made very quickly, but also resulting in a smooth and gradual transition of color from light to dark.

The effect is achieved by blending clay on a diagonal bias. This can be done with an acrylic roller, but the process is much easier and faster with a clay-dedicated pasta machine.

The technique involves blending clay triangles (two right-angle triangles for two-color blends and a combination of right-angle triangles on the outside and isosceles triangles for interior clay sections for multiple-color blends).

The end result is a color gradient sheet that can be used a number of ways. One of the most common is to stretch the blended sheet thinner and thinner (typically on the fifth- or sixth-largest setting of the pasta machine) lengthwise and rolling it into a log. This is one type of "bull's-eye cane" (a "cane" is a log of clay). The sheet can be rolled from dark to light or light to dark depending on the desired use.

Other options include using the sheet as is in thick or thinned applications for backgrounds. These are beautiful for journal covers or for wrapping around bakeable vessels. Yet another use is to make gradient loaves | see GRADIENT LOAVES, page 43 |.

The greater the contrast between the colors being blended, the more folded passes through the pasta machine are required to achieve a complete blend. Typically, a high-contrast blend (for example, white to black) will require 25 to 30 passes through the machine's largest setting, and a lower-contrast blend (for example, white to yellow) will require 10 to 15 passes. It's not necessary to count the passes. You'll know when you're satisfied with the results.

Creating incomplete blends is a great way to get special effects in bull's-eye canes. The result can appear somewhat striated or veined, resembling the look of Ikat fabric. Another alternative is to introduce thin strips of other clay colors to incomplete blends or add inclusions such as glitter into the clay for unique effects.

It would be possible to devote an entire book to variations, projects, and applications involving the Skinner Blend. In this book, we'll just cover the tip of the proverbial iceberg in hopes you'll be inspired not only to master this technique but also to experiment further.

TECHNIQUE #1

Basic Skinner Blending

Some people begin their blends with triangles cut from squares, and others from rectangles. Either method will work in creating your blend. On that note, I realize that what works best for me is not always the best or easiest method for everyone.

If, in working with this or any other recommendation, you find a better, faster, or easier method for yourself, then that will, of course, be the right way.

1 Cut a 3-in. by 4½-in. template from an index card. Larger rectangles or even squares can be cut from an index card to create a larger blended sheet. Cut out two rectangles of contrasting colored clay from sheets rolled through the largest setting of the pasta machine.

It's important to start with a sufficient amount of clay in order to have enough to repeatedly fold in half, as the clay lengthens during the blending process. A half-block minimum per color is recommended for getting started.

2 Cut each rectangle diagonally with the clay blade. This can be done from corner to corner for a more subtle end result. For a more dramatic effect, offset the diagonal cut ⅛ in. from each opposing corner. This will leave some of each original color at each end of the completed blend, giving a more dramatic gradation between colors.

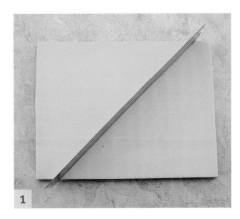

3 Stack the same color triangles, one over the other, to create double-thick triangles of clay. Make sure the wide and narrow ends of each triangle are layered to match identically **a**. Align the two double-thick triangles together to reform a rectangle with both colors as shown **b**. Run this clay rectangle through the pasta machine on the largest setting.

4 Fold the flattened rectangle in half and run it through the largest setting of the machine **a**. It's important when creating any Skinner Blend that the side edges of clay (after folding before each pass) are identical in color (that is, yellow is touching only yellow along the outer folded edges, and blue is touching only blue on the opposite side) **b**.

The other tip is that after folding the clay, both or all colors touch the rollers lengthwise during every pass. The clay should also always be inserted fold first into the pasta machine to avoid trapping air between the layers.

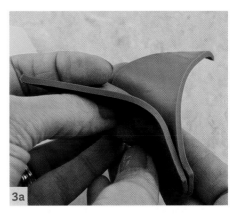

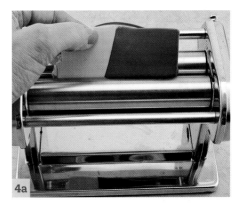

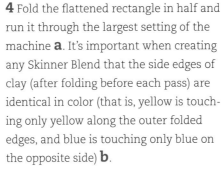

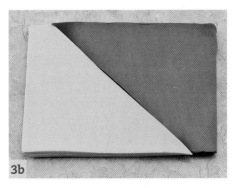

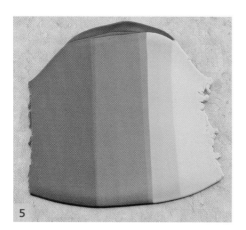

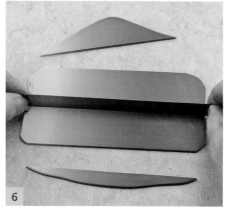

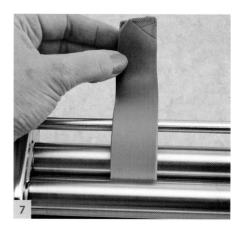

This is the blend after only five passes. You can begin to see the gradation.

note

On some machines, the clay sheet will come out wider than when it went in. This is from being compressed during rolling. Simply fold the sheet in half as directed on page 39 and slightly scrunch it together to reduce the width, making it the right size to be placed back through the rollers.

5 Repeat Step 4 as many times as it takes to get a smooth gradient effect. During the first several passes, it won't look like this is being accomplished, but the effect will begin to reveal itself as you continue to roll through. Remember, this can take as few as 10 passes or as many as 30.

6 Once you are satisfied with the blend, it's time to stretch the sheet (unless a thicker background sheet is desired). It's always easier to work or manipulate a short, wide cane than a long, narrow one. Since the sheet doesn't come out uniform and even, you may need to trim a little off the edges. Cut the sheet in half lengthwise and stack one half over the other to create a strip of double thickness.

7 Roll the strip lengthwise through the largest setting of the pasta machine. Maintain control over the sheet while stretching by gently holding and guiding it through the rollers during this stage. Repeatedly run the clay lengthwise through the pasta machine, adjusting the rollers to increasingly thinner settings with each pass until you have rolled the sheet through the fifth- or sixth-largest settings.

If making a bull's-eye cane, decide whether you want the cane to go from light to dark or dark to light starting from the center core of the cane.

Start by rolling the core color in on itself as you would roll a jelly roll cake. Continue rolling until the sheet is formed into a log. Air pockets can ruin a millefiori cane by creating distortion.

note

Some brands of polymer clay are stickier than others before curing and may need to be fed out the bottom of the machine onto your work surface when stretching. Make sure your work area is clean of debris before doing this in order to avoid contaminating the sheet. Also, do not allow the clay to sit on the roller guard plates when cranking, as it may result in the strip sticking and tearing.

tip

To make starting the roll easier, make a thin snake from the clay color that will form the center core. Place this along the end of the stretched sheet and roll the clay over the snake to make it easier to start a tight, compact roll (see the top photo below).

At the opposite end, trim a straight edge, cutting away any excess or jagged clay. If the color doesn't extend all the way around the outer clay layer of the roll, add a sheet of the end color from one that's been rolled through the last setting used to stretch the sheet. Trim the excess clay. Compress the cane, starting at the center (see "Cane Reduction" on page 49) and roll while rotating with your fingers to compact and compress any air out of the center.

TECHNIQUE #2

Multiple-Color Skinner Blending

1 Make an index card template with 3 or more colors. Use the template when cutting out the colors you will be using for your triple-blended gradient.

2 Gently compress the triangles together with your fingers. Fold these in half and repeatedly roll through the largest setting of the pasta machine following the directions for Steps 4 through 6 for Basic Skinner Blending **a, b**.

3 For a bull's-eye cane trim, stack, and stretch the multicolored gradient sheet as explained in Basic Skinner Blending or use one of the other techniques explained in the pages that follow.

More dramatic jelly-roll canes can be made from gradient Skinner Blended sheets that are not stretched.

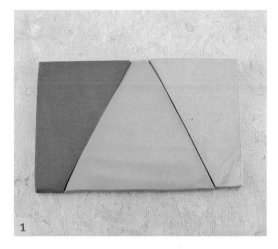

2a

1

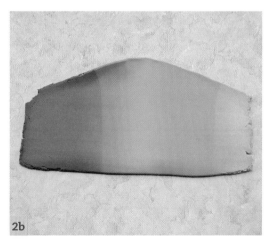

2b

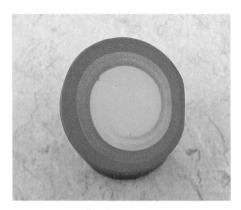

This jelly-roll cane made with the thickest setting shows more pronounced striations than would be seen in a cane made from a stretched, thin sheet.

Notice how much more dramatic Variation 1 becomes when a strip of black clay from the sixth-largest setting of the pasta machine is placed over the strip before rolling.

VARIATION 1

To make a jelly-roll cane with a subtle striated effect, follow Step 6 of Basic Skinner Blending to create a stacked strip of double thickness. Roll this stacked strip lengthwise through only the largest setting of the machine to stretch and elongate the strip. Follow by rolling from light to dark or dark to light as desired.

Diagram A

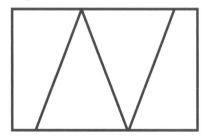

Diagram B

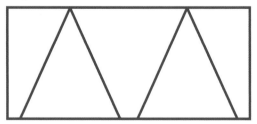

VARIATION 2

A more dramatic jelly-roll cane can be achieved simply by placing a thin layer of contrasting clay (rolled through the fifth- or sixth-largest setting of the pasta machine) on top of the gradient clay strip made in Variation 1, and then rolling. Play with clay colors using either a color used in your blend or a completely different color from one in the blend. Experiment with color contrasts from extreme to subtle and the thicknesses of this layered sheet for different effects. You can even layer thin and thick gradient sheets over another gradient sheet for different looks.

For four- or five-color gradient blends, refer to diagrams A and B for cutting angles.

Creating Surface Sheets

Working with blended clay sheeting is a great way to create beautiful backgrounds in your work, whether for jewelry, home décor, or accessory making. Gradient clay sheets can also be enlarged and extended by backing them with thicker layers of white clay, followed by rolling through thinner settings of the pasta machine or with an acrylic roller. Only white clay is recommended when backing the gradient sheet for enlarging this surface since stretching the clay will also thin it, allowing the underlying layer to mute the surface color.

Another method for making larger blended sheets is to connect multiple sheets. To do this seamlessly, abut the sides to be connected at opposing 45-degree angles and join the ends so that they connect at the beveled edges (see diagram C). This also works for overlapping single-color clay sheets.

Consider adding texture to your blended backgrounds using coarse sandpaper, rubber texture plates, and more.

Diagram C

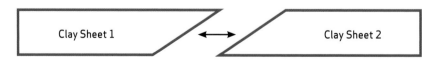

Clay Sheet 1   Clay Sheet 2

Gradient Loaves

These formations of gradient blends are ideal when a smaller background sheet is needed for applications requiring a vertical blend as opposed to a cylindrical formation like the one created with a bull's-eye cane. Loaf formations are also ideal when making blends of three colors or more **1**.

Slices from these loaves can also be enlarged, as with surface sheets. When extending loaf slices, you may notice a more striated look as the clay stretches, as opposed to the effect you get using larger, just-blended sheets. Texturing the clay surface when creating your project can minimize this result.

Stretch the clay as instructed in Steps 6 and 7 of the Basic Skinner Blending instructions. Cut a clean, straight edge along one end of the strip. Fold the clay back and forth like an accordion in ½-in.- to 1-in.-wide intervals. Do not press the clay together too firmly while doing this. Once the clay has been completely folded, trim the excess clay off at the opposite end of the strip. Gently compress the stack together with your fingers or an acrylic roller to remove any air pockets **2**.

tip

You can trim the loaf from the sides and the back, but you'll have larger workable surface areas if you leave these distorted sides intact. Leaving the back end untrimmed will also give you more of an anchor when slicing the last bit of loaf, leaving you more usable clay.

Ribbons

Compressing gradient loaves and assembling them together with the lightest sides facing inward achieves the illusion of a satin ribbon or reflective strip **1**. Elongated and stretched ribbon canes can be cut and assembled with vertical lines opposing horizontal lines in a checkerboard fashion, which can mimic the appearance of basket-woven designs **2**.

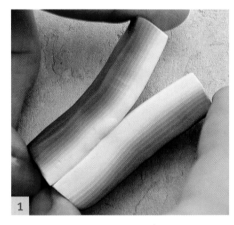

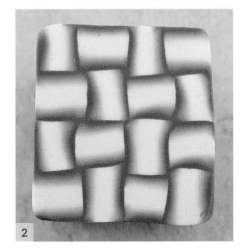

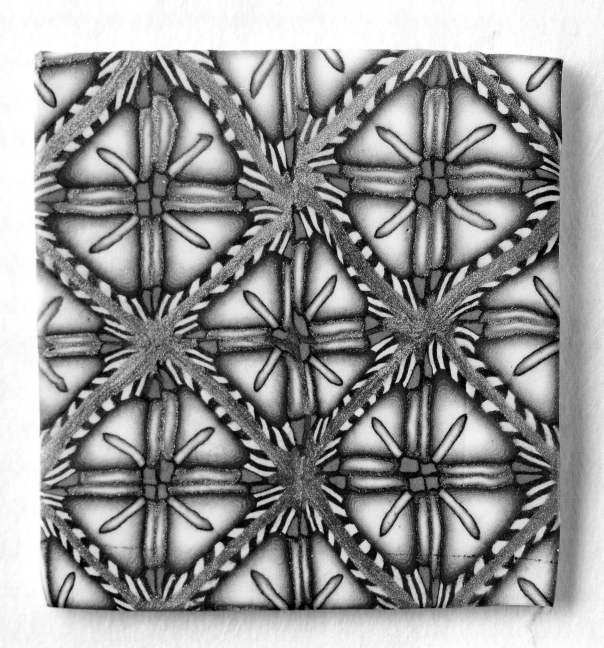

CHAPTER FOUR

Millefiori Caning

ONE OF THE MOST POPULAR TECHNIQUES (and the most intimidating) is millefiori caning. This is a process based on the ancient Roman glass technique that creates a horizontal rod of single or multiple components that form an image, pattern, or picture. This can be as simple as the gradient bull's-eye cane taught in Basic Skinner Blending (see chapter 3).

Don't let the idea of a complex cane intimidate you. While there are varying degrees of complexity, some of the cane tutorials in this chapter will yield amazingly intricate-looking canes that require neither years of skill nor precision. This chapter is an introduction to the concept on the most basic of levels and offers a handful of designs with wide application and ease of variation.

TECHNIQUES

- Striped Jelly-Roll Canes
- Leaf Canes
- Flower Canes
- Gradient Checkerboard Canes
- Gradient Heart Canes
- Smoosh Canes
- Junk Canes

The original concept of caning is thousands of years old and can be seen in ancient beads and artwork found in Europe and Africa. These days, millefiori technique shows up in some surprising places aside from glass and clay work. Without realizing it, you may have seen it in candles that have exterior designs reminiscent of stained glass. The patterns on the outer veneer are made through combination extrusions of colored wax rods.

This technique is also used in the making of hard and soft candies. As a child, you may have enjoyed taffy with an American flag or a holiday tree that appeared on both sides of the candy. These are created by combining and extruding colored rods and ribbons of candy into logs, which are sliced into individual pieces. Some of the more contemporary uses of millefiori technique are found in soap making, cheese, and ready-to-bake cookie dough that features holiday patterns, which are revealed when sliced for baking.

One way to think of millefiori is to regard it as the sculpting of an image along a horizontal plane. The assembly of multiple-colored components into a combination forms a rod, or "cane." These components can vary from round snakes and flat strips to square or triangular logs. When this rod is sliced crosswise with a blade, the pattern made by the chosen assembly method can be seen wherever the cane is sliced. The cane can be reduced in size by hand or tool manipulation (see page 49 for more information on reduction), yet the image remains intact throughout the cane, no matter how small the diameter.

This sunflower cane was made by combining both veined and plain Skinner Blended bull's-eye canes.

Helpful Caning Pointers

- Canes can be made small or large, depending on the number of slices desired. Commercially produced canes are made and measured in pounds. It's best, however, to always start assembling components of at least 1-in. lengths. Shorter lengths can make assembling more detailed patterns difficult.

- All methods used to compact and reduce a cane will result in some distortion along the ends. This is normal. The better you become at reduction through practice, the less distortion you will have to cut from your cane ends. Even though there is no waste in clay, you'll want to improve your reduction technique in order to have the maximum length of usable cane possible.

- Although various brands of clay can be blended and baked together, I recommend making canes using the same brand of clay to ensure uniform consistency. Since there are great differences among clay brands in firmness and elasticity, using assorted brands of clay in a single cane can result in a great deal of distortion. If mixing brands cannot be avoided, mix equal ratios of brands for each and every color that is used in the creation of a cane.

Slices from millefiori canes can be used a number of different ways. Thicker slices can be pierced through the center or sides for use as buttons or beads. Thinner slices are typically applied over base layers of clay to create veneers for decorating any number of surfaces.

If you're new to caning, my best advice is to start with simple canes, following some of the guidelines in this chapter, and work your way into more complex caning. Practice and mastery of the basics will serve you well as you build your caning skill.

My very first attempts were extremely complex canes. I spent eight hours on my first cane, not really knowing how to properly reduce it, and ended up with a mess. I was so frustrated, I didn't attempt caning of any sort for several years. Knowing what I know now, I could have turned that mess into a complex kaleidoscope cane that could have been quite lovely. Sadly, it ended up being blended together for armature clay, which wasn't a total waste, but eight hours is a lot of time to spend on filler.

Work your way up to larger or more complex canes gradually (like the cross section of the face that can be seen here). Typically, complex canes involve many different sections assembled to form detailed pictorial images. These often incorporate shading through use of gradient blended canes, loaves, and sheets to add depth and realism to a two-dimensional plane.

Even simple canes will amaze your friends and family when you explain that they are not painted, but actual assemblies of individually colored clays you created by hand.

Most brands of clay will be too soft immediately after caning to slice with good results. For this reason, I recommend allowing your cane to rest for several hours or even days before slicing. As the clay sits, it will regain firmness, making it easier to get clean, crisp slices. The sharper the blade, the better!

For those who just can't wait, create your canes with clay that has less blade resistance or drag, or freeze your cane for 10 to 15 minutes before slicing. Clay thaws quickly, so repeat freezing may be required for larger canes.

- All clays, including canes, will become stiffer over time so the storage period for canes made from the firmest brands of clay is shorter than that of less firm clays. Over the course of months or years, canes made from firmer clays may not be malleable after slicing

unless the cane is warmed throughout. This typically involves reducing the cane to recondition it.

Attempting to roll or thin a slice from an older cane made from firm clay may result in fracture of the clay. This shouldn't be a problem when thicker slices are cut for the use of buttons or beads. In this instance, drilling holes is best done after baking.

When the reduction of cane size is not desirable, constructing canes from softer brands of clay may work best. Creating canes from soft clay requires a very light touch and may be difficult for those with very warm hands.

- Storing canes is fairly easy. They do not need to be wrapped, but they should be stored in the types of plastic containers mentioned in chapter 1 to protect them from airborne particles and kept away from heat and light when not in use.

- When creating a complex cane, it may be helpful to sketch the pattern onto paper first. The pattern can then be enlarged or reduced on a photocopier or scanner as desired and placed under clear, tempered glass to use as a template when creating and assembling the components.

- Bake clay slices for beads and buttons on stiff cardboard to prevent shiny spots from forming on the underlying side.

Cane Shapes

Finished canes can be round, square, triangular, rectangular, hexagonal, or dimensional. Once created, many canes can be reshaped through compression by hand or roller to form new shapes. Straight-sided cane shapes (square, rectangular, or triangular) can be aligned side by side over underlying clay or another bakeable surface and rolled until melded into a seamless surface to create repeating patterns. Round or odd-shaped canes can be sliced and placed over contrasting clay surfaces to achieve polka-dotted or random pattern effects.

PACKING

Packing dimensional crevices and curves along the exterior of a cane is one way to give the cane a reducible shape. When packed cane slices are embedded onto a clay surface with an identical color used to fill the background, the cane will appear to float on the background surface, as if it were painted on. If the

packing clay color differs from the background color of clay the slice is being embedded into, it will highlight the slice against the background.

WORKING IN EXACT SIZE

When a dimensional cane shape is desired without the use of packing, one option is to create and assemble the components to the exact size that is desired. Great attention to packing and compression must be made during the assembly process to prevent visible gaps from forming between components. Shaped, dimensional canes should be allowed to rest for several days so the clay can firm up. Slicing must be done carefully to prevent distorting the clay shape. Artist Lynne Ann Schwarzenberg slices her canes while standing them vertically, rather than laying them down, to prevent distortion.

PACKING WITH TRANSLUCENT CLAY

Another method to create cane slices that can float on any background color is to pack the exterior of a cane with translucent clay until it can be made into a round or square cane. When canes are reduced to the desired size, you can slice away the translucent clay from the exterior in short increments (¼-in. to ½-in. sections at a time). This will expose the cane so that you can take dimensional slices that won't have visible wrapping.

Cane Reduction

Cane reduction is an essential component of creating successful millefiori canes, and it is especially crucial to remove any air trapped between components. Failure to properly reduce a cane will result in the cane falling apart if rolled to reduce, internal distortion of the pattern, or gaps and/or holes in the cane slices.

As the name implies, the method reduces the overall size of the finished cane. Keep this in mind when constructing your canes. The beautiful thing about caning is that you can divide a single cane into identical canes of various sizes.

The methods for reducing canes include one or more of the following manipulations: hand compression/squeezing, stretching, and rolling across the work surface or with a rod. Many people incorporate various combinations of these methods in the reduction of a cane. Like anything else, practice will improve your reduction skills and help you determine the method that works best for you.

A round cane, like the one pictured on page 50, is compressed in the middle by squeezing between the thumb and index fingers while frequently rotating to keep the reduction consistent on all sides. When the cane begins to take on an hourglass shape, work your way toward one end using the same method of reduction. Then, turn the cane around

note

Very thin slices of lighter-colored clay laid over a dark background may become somewhat muted in tone, as the color of the veneer layer can show through. Use white or light clay as a backing.

and work your way down the opposite end until the diameter is uniform. Follow with stretching until the cane is nearly the desired diameter. Finish by lightly rolling the cane over the work surface until smooth.

Reducing a cane by rolling it with your fingers or the palms of your hands should be done very minimally. Rolling can twist and distort a design internally. That isn't a problem with simpler canes such as bull's-eyes and spirals. Rely primarily on rotational squeezing and/or stretching by hand until the cane is the desired size and shape. Refining square, rectangular, and triangular canes can be done with an acrylic rod.

Cane Slicing

Cane slicing is best done with clean, sharp blades. Blades with debris on them or older blades with notching along the

edge will result in drag lines appearing across your slices. To cut thin, even slices when slicing canes, sit up straight. Look down directly over the top edge of the clay blade to make sure it is perpendicular with your vision and is straight up and down as you slice.

ROUND

When cutting a round cane, roll the blade back and forth as if you were sawing a log. This will also cause the cane to rotate, reducing the tendency to flatten on one side.

SQUARE AND RECTANGLE

Cut into square and rectangular canes by starting with a few sawing motions, and then slice straight down once the blade has entered the cane. Rotate the cane one quarter turn after each slice to help maintain the shape.

TRIANGULAR

For triangular canes, cut straight down through the upper tip. Rotate the triangle to the next side after each turn to maintain the shape.

TEARDROP SHAPED

Slice teardrop-shaped canes by starting at the round, wide end and slicing the blade downward toward the tip at an angle. Think of this motion like that of a skier making his or her way downhill. Flip the cane over after each slice to help maintain the teardrop shape.

It can be helpful to form what is called a "cane trough" for slicing round or

dimensional canes with less distortion. From uncured clay, create a channel that conforms to the shape of the bottom of your cane. Lay the cane on the trough and adjust it so that the desired amount extends beyond the channel, and slice. Create the trough using a clay color that matches the outer color of the cane to prevent contrasting residue from contaminating your slices.

It may be helpful to mark the desired slicing widths on the cane before cutting. You can eyeball these dimensions, use a ruler, or use a clay-marking tool found at many craft and hobby stores. I like to use hair combs with varying widths between the teeth. Lightly press whichever tool you are using along the outside of the cane to guide you. There are also professional cane-cutting slicers and guides that can be found through Internet searches and clay suppliers.

Thin slices are typically used for rolling until embedded on a clay veneer sheet or sliced thicker for use as dimensional accents, beads, or buttons.

Cane Techniques

The following methods are just the beginning of what you can create with the millefiori cane concept. Additional resources for more in-depth caning concepts can be found via Internet searches, bookstores, and libraries. Guilds, stores, and creative organizations throughout the world host classes in polymer clay millefiori caning. The trick is to get comfortable with basic concepts and expand on them by combining technique and experimentation once you feel confident with the more elementary formations featured in this chapter.

There are many more possibilities for creating jelly-roll canes than can be featured in a single book. Two types of gradient jelly-roll canes were reviewed in chapter 3, on Skinner Blending. Here is yet another version of the jelly-roll cane that offers a whimsical look to your creations.

TECHNIQUE #1

Striped Jelly-Roll Canes

1 Select two or more colors to make a striped loaf | see instructions in the SUSPENDED CRYSTAL PENDANT project, page 160 |. The number of layers, the colors, and the thickness of each clay sheet will all affect the finished appearance of your jelly roll. Play with varying thicknesses, too, in creating these fun canes.

2 Cut thick, uniform slices from the loaf with a clay blade. Again, the thickness of these slices will determine the look of your cane. Lay these abutted side by side with the striped pattern alternating along a thin (fourth- to sixth-largest setting of the pasta machine) strip of contrasting colored clay that is 3 in. to 6 in. long. The width of the strip should match the length of the striped slices.

3 Cut a 45-degree angle along one end with the clay blade.

4 Bend the edge of the background strip up and over to form a curl. Continue to roll the entire strip of striped clay until you are satisfied with the number of rotations in the cane.

TECHNIQUE #2

Leaf Canes

There are thousands of possibilities for creating both realistic and imaginary leaf canes. Here we feature three types of leaves, from a very basic and a slightly more complex version of the same concept to a much more involved formation.

A simple leaf cane can be made very quickly from wrapped or gradient bull's-eyes.

1 Stand a bull's-eye cane on its end and slice it in half down the middle with a clay blade.

2 Roll out a sheet of contrasting color to use as the leaf's vein. The sheet should be very thin (using the fifth- or sixth-largest setting of the pasta machine). Cut a straight edge along the end of the clay sheet after trimming it as wide as the cane's length.

Insert it halfway across one of the sliced cane halves. Reattach the other half of the cane and compress the cane together firmly before reducing.

3 When the cane is reduced to the desired diameter, pinch the end of the cane on the side opposite the vein line that is pointed up. Turn the cane around and repeat pinching the opposite end to begin forming the teardrop shape.

4 Check that the pinched ends are aligned parallel to one another. If they are not, this indicates that twisting occurred during rolling. If this has happened, twist one end to align it parallel to the other end and pinch the rest of the cane between these two points.

Hold the cane in the air while doing this step. Allowing the cane to rest on the work surface will create a triangle and not a teardrop shape, which forms the leaf.

5 Note the instructions in the Cane Slicing section on page 50 when working with teardrop canes **a**.

Taking the basic leaf to the next step is an easy variation of the previous leaf cane, and offers a more detailed appearance for your work.

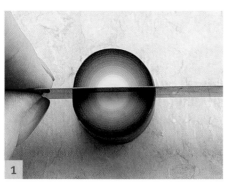
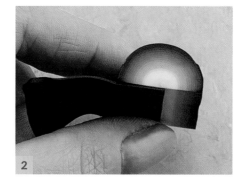

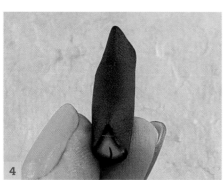

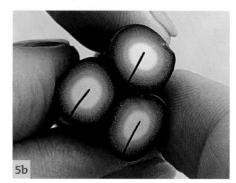

Create a veined cane as described on the facing page and reduce it to at least 3 in. in length. Cut it into even sections and stack one piece over two. All the sections should have the vein line facing upward. Compress and reduce to the desired diameter. Shape the cane following Steps 3 and 4 of the basic leaf **b**.

Have fun with inventive leaf concepts. Use striping for vein lines, implement the use of a wavy blade to open a cane for lining with solid and Skinner Blended clay sheets, and experiment to formulate your own unique leaf patterns.

This complex leaf cane is just the beginning of the options open to the imaginative clayer. The concept offers a more varied approach to gradient blending than those found in chapter 3.

1 Roll out three colors of clay on the largest setting of the pasta machine. Cut two sheets each from the darkest color

(1 in. by 3 in.) for a total of four sheets. Roll one 1-in. by 3-in. sheet of the lightest-color clay on the thickest setting of the machine. Stack the five sheets as shown.

2 Roll the clay through the largest setting of the pasta machine to meld the strips together.

3 Cut thin ½-in.- to 1-in.-long strips of white clay from a sheet rolled through the largest setting of the pasta machine. Place these randomly over the clay surface, all pointed vertically (the direction the clay is going to be rolled through the machine).

4 Roll the clay sheet through the largest setting of the pasta machine. Cut the sheet in half lengthwise, stack, and roll through the largest setting. Repeat this step two more times. Cut the sheet in half and stack, then in half again.

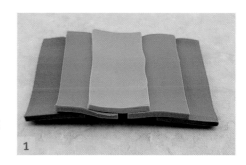

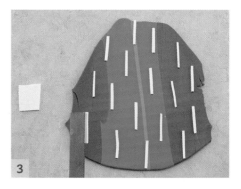

Note the complexity achieved by laying leaf cane slices in a tip-over-end scallop fashion along the edge of this decorative platter.

5 Compress the darker ends of the stack inward with your hands until a square-shaped plug is formed. Use your fingers to shape it into a cylinder and lightly roll it across your work surface to round it.

6 Cut a piece of gold clay that's been rolled through the third-largest setting of the pasta machine to the width and half the diameter of the cane. Wrap this on three sides with a sheet of black clay rolled through the sixth-largest setting of the pasta machine. Pinch the wrapped end of the gold clay to taper it to a point.

7 Slice the cane down the middle (as with the basic leaf shape) and insert the wrapped gold clay vein halfway along the cane end as shown, with the pinched end inward. Fit the two halves together and compress firmly. Trim any excess veining if needed.

8 Wrap the cane with black clay rolled through the fifth-largest setting of the pasta machine.

9 When the cane is the desired diameter, pinch to shape. Leaf canes don't necessarily have to be a teardrop shape. As with this leaf, both ends were pinched to form more of a blade leaf shape. Also try punching thin slices cut from canes with leaf-shaped cutters or by pressing into leaf molds.

Flower Canes

Just as with leaves, flower canes can be realistic or imaginary formations. They can be constructed with as little as a single petal (for calla lilies), a few petals (for tulips), or many, many more (for sunflowers and daises). The use of gradient blended elements (bull's-eyes and sheets for striping) is a great way to get your flower cane creations to really pop.

The nine-petal flower cane shown on page 46 begins with two bull's-eye canes.

1 Cut 1½-in.-long by ¾-in.-diameter gradient bull's-eye cane into quarters through the center as shown in the top left photo on the facing page.

2 Pinch each quarter into elongated teardrops with the lighter end being the tapered point. Assemble the four darker teardrops (lightest color facing inward) in alternating rows against three of the lighter cane quarters. Stretch and reduce the remaining lighter-colored teardrop section to 1½ in. long and set aside for the next step.

3 Compress and reduce the cane to 3 in. long with your fingers. Cut this in half and reassemble side by side with the fourth lighter teardrop (which was set aside on the last step), bridging the two halves together as shown in the bottom left photo on the facing page.

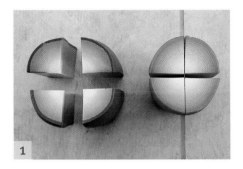

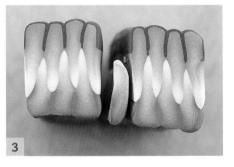

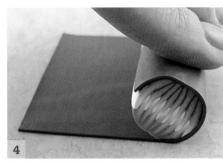

tip

Packing the cane with a background color will fill the crevices and allow the cane to retain its shape during reduction and slicing. Triangular wedges were made from a clay snake and packed into the space between.

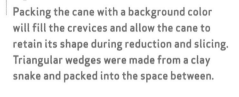

Here you can see what reduced slices look like on the matching background veneer used to make this bead (above).

4 Compress the cane inward to form a square shape and then round the edges with your fingers. Roll the cane to make it round and wrap it in a sheet of the darkest color used. A medium-thick to thin setting should be used for this sheet, depending on how prominent you want the outline of the petal to appear.

5 Compress, stretch, and roll the cane to 7 in. long. Cut off the distorted ends. Cut the remaining cane into six equal lengths. Pinch the lighter end (or darker if you prefer, but all sections should be pinched along the same side) into a teardrop shape. Press the tapered end down against the work surface to slightly flatten. Place the narrow end of the tear-

drops against a round center cane with a diameter that is approximately one-third the length of the teardrops.

6 Lightly compress the cane to compact it and fuse the components together. You have several options for use now including packing with a translucent clay or background clay color.

note

A gradient jelly-roll cane was used for this center (below).

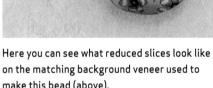

3

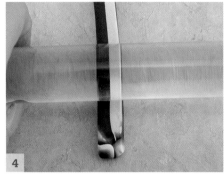

4

5

TECHNIQUE #4

Gradient Checkerboard Canes

The simple combination of reversed gradient blended bull's-eye canes can be used to create a stunning checkerboard effect.

1 Cut a Skinner Blended sheet (as described in chapter 3) in half before thinning through the pasta machine. Thin each half as described in the basic bull's-eye directions on page 41. Roll one strip from light to dark, and the other from dark to light.

2 Roll and reduce each bull's-eye cane to approximately 5 in. in length. The diameter of each cane should be identical to one another. Cut off the distorted ends and align the canes side by side.

3 Cut the length in half. Flip one half over 180 degrees and place directly over the top of the bottom cane halves.

4 Compress and reduce the combined clay sections with your fingers, starting from the middle or center and gradually

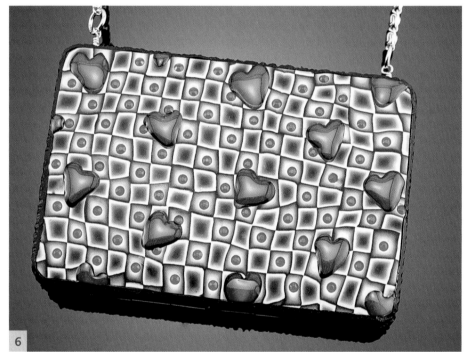

6

working your way out to one end, using slow, deliberate pressure while rotating the clay. When one end matches the diameter of the center of the cane, flip it over and work from the center to compress and reduce out toward the other end. Use the acrylic rod to further reduce, compress, and shape the cane to 7 in. in length.

5 Trim off the distorted ends and cut the cane into four equal lengths. Assemble these together with the square colors, alternating to form a 16-block checkerboard.

6 Slices of the cane can be aligned side by side over a surface to create a larger checkerboard area.

Gradient Heart Canes

This is a very simple cane to create for accents.

Roll a plain wrapped or gradient bull's-eye cane to the desired size. Pinch into a teardrop shape. Indent and shape the end opposite the tapered teardrop point using a knitting needle. The cane can be sliced as you would a teardrop shape or packed with filler clay to make a reducible cane.

Smoosh Canes

This is a foolproof method for taking the complexity out of complex caning. I also like to call this "tie-dye cane," since I find that some of the assemblies possible are similar to patterns found in the fabric-dyeing technique made popular in the 1960s.

This is a cane I developed that yields amazingly complex-looking results with very little effort. I've taught this over and over to people who have never worked with clay before. Most will complain along the way that their cane is disastrous and that they must be doing it wrong. There is nothing like the pleasure and surprise experienced when they first cut into the finished cane and see how beautiful their cane turned out.

This is an especially fun and easy technique, as it only requires your hands, a roller, and a blade. We'll examine mirror canes (four-section assemblies) and kaleidoscope canes made using the same basic construction.

1 Begin with four quarter blocks of differently colored clay (three colors can also be used to make five-column canes with this technique that are a bit simpler). Two colors should be in high contrast to one another.

Roll each color into ¼-in.-diameter snakes. Neatness and uniformity are not important in this step. Each snake should be 9 in. or longer. Pinch the clay snake

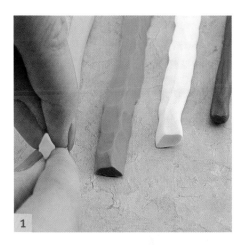

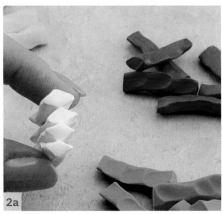

between both thumbs and forefingers. This will form the diameter into a smooshed diamond shape. Do this along the entire length of each clay snake and cut each into 1-in. to 1½-in. lengths.

2 Build up a column of four pieces of the same color of clay **a**. You can start with either the lightest or the darkest color. This will form V-shaped channels on either side of each piece. Wedge diamond-shaped sections from a high-contrast color in the channels on either side of the

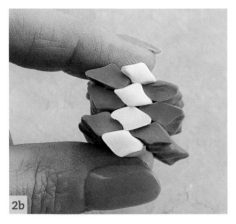

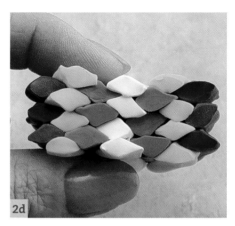

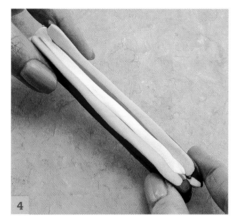

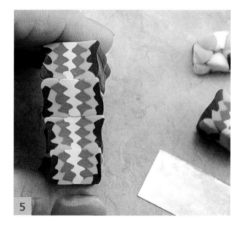

center column **b**. While the clay is being handled, it's common for the channels to become compressed together. Use your fingers or any clay tool to reopen these as needed when adding new components.

It doesn't matter if distortion occurs during this process. In fact, it can enhance the finished cane, but it is important that the sections interlock or overlap with the clay sections on either side.

Here you can see the rows being added, color by color, until a loaf of interlocking diamond components is created **c, d**.

3 Compress the block into a rectangular shape.

4 Use your hands to further compress to reduce and lengthen the cane to

7 in. long. Slightly flatten the cane with a roller until it is about ½ in. to ¾ in. thick.

5 Trim off the distorted ends. Cut the cane into four equal sections and stack one over the other. Do not try to match the patterns. The less perfect the assembly is, the more interesting the finished pattern will be.

6a

6b

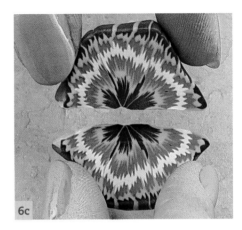

6c

6d

6e

6 Compress the stack until it is a square shape **a**. Reduce it to 7 in. long again. Cut off the distorted ends. You now have several options for creating kaleidoscope canes (made up of six equilateral triangles, or three diamonds), mirror canes (made up of four mirrored sections that mirror along four sides), or continuous-border canes (made up of two matching panels). Here are a few samples that can be achieved with this cane:

Pinch the cane into a triangle shape. Cut into three equal lengths and assemble in a fanlike semicircle **b**.

Cut the cane in half and match the two pieces to form a kaleidoscope cane. Pinching the cane with the column rows facing horizontally will result in a look different than that of a cane whose design is pinched vertically) **c, d**.

To make a mirror cane, shape the entire clay length (from Step 4) into a triangle shape. Cut the cane in half and mirror two ends. The cane will now have a diamond shape.

Compress the points of the diamond inward along the entire length to form a square shape. Mirror four square sections to form your cane design. Refine the cane with a roller so that it is uniform **e**.

The variations of this concept are totally limitless, so have fun coming up with your own "smoosh" manipulations.

Here are two examples of what assembly of the square cane will look like when mirrored. The version on the right is simply a reversal of the pattern all four components face when assembled. Once again, pinching the cane in the opposite direction will result in a completely different pattern when assembled.

Junk Canes

There are lots of wonderful uses for clay left over from your projects. We'll have a chance to consider other options for utilizing clay scraps in other chapters as well.

Scrap clay and cane ends that have black, brown, or gray often don't blend into aesthetically pleasing colors when completely mixed together (and clayers often have an overabundance of them), but they can work well in canes. Options for scrap or junk clay include creating Mokumé Gané blocks, armature, blending for mold making, or extending background clay sheets.

Being able to turn this type of scrap into a cane once again proves that polymer clay is a very affordable medium to work with. There never needs to be any waste with clay.

Set aside small scraps and cane ends and store in bags of complementary color combinations. This way, you can organize the clay until you have enough to make these canes.

Depending on the colors combined, the resulting looks can resemble stained glass, insect wings, or tortoiseshell. Also use the basic formation to combine solid and gradient bull's-eye canes to create a variety of canes from citrus fruit cross-sections to fairy wings.

1 Start with a ball of scraps that is at least the size of a golf ball or small plum. Compress the scraps tightly to make sure there is no air inside and the clay is soft and pliable. Do not mix in any way that will blend the colors together. If the colors in your mix are predominantly dark, chop the ball up and add several chopped pieces of light-colored clay to lighten and increase the contrast of the mix. Compress the ball back together tightly.

2 Roll or stretch the ball of clay into a short, wide snake about 3 in. long. Trim the ends with the clay blade. Wrap the short snake you just made with a layer of contrasting clay (black or white) that has been rolled out on the third-largest setting of the pasta machine.

3 Roll and reduce the wrapped snake to 8 in. long. Slightly flatten the cane along the entire length. Trim away the distorted ends and divide the snake into seven 1-in.-long sections.

Assemble the sections as shown: two sets of two pieces compressed together with a single piece placed vertically on each side of these sets. Compress this assembly together by hand to form a square cane.

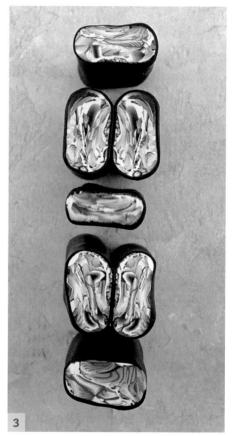

4 Shape the square cane into a triangular shape by pinching along the entire length of one side between your fingers. Do this along either side that is lined (not the smooth side). Rotate the cane repeatedly while pinching it into shape.

5 Reduce and lengthen the cane to 5 in. long by stretching, continually rotating and refining with your fingers. Cut off the distorted ends and divide into three equal pieces.

6 Assemble a semicircle with the three tips facing inward.

7 Cut this in half and press the halves together.

8 This cane can be used for round slices or reshaped for repeating-tile patterns.

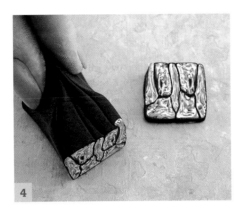

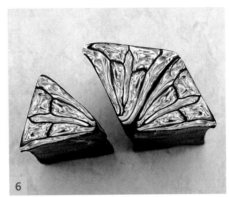

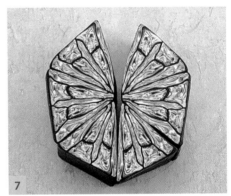

CHAPTER FIVE

Image Transfers

ADDING DETAILED IMAGES TO POLYMER CLAY is a wonderful way to create focal pieces or decorative elements. I particularly love the look of image transfers in collaged clay work.

Some methods, like toner-based and pencil transfers, actually embed the image into the clay's surface, while others, including waterslide transfers, apply photo-quality images on top of the surface. This chapter features some of the fastest, easiest, and most tried-and-true methods for getting images transferred onto your polymer clay surfaces.

Some images will be applied face down onto clay and others face up. When the former is required, use whatever method is needed to reverse your image if it contains text, otherwise it will appear backward when transferred.

TECHNIQUES

- Waterslide Transfers
- Custom Inkjet Transfers
- Preprinted Waterslide Transfers
- Stamps as Transfers
- Liquid Clay Transfers
- Toner-Based Transfers
- Coloring Toner Transfers
- Deli Paper Transfers

Waterslide Transfers

They say necessity is the mother of invention; frustration is more like it. Several years ago, I found that the success I had in transferring colored-toner photocopies was no longer working consistently (or at all) with copies I was making. Even when the method worked, I still found the technique very labor intensive and fussy, as using too much pressure during the application process could easily damage the image.

In teaching this method, I found it was very difficult for some people to get satisfactory results. This, combined with the changes in toner inks, prompted me to search for an easier and faster method of getting foolproof results. This led to the introduction of my inkjet waterslide paper for clay and crafting.

The material works much like the decals that are found in model airplane and car kits. The beauty of this product is that anyone can custom-print his or her own photos, artwork, sayings, or clip art using a home inkjet printer. With com-

Clockwise from top left: Waterslide transfer over white clay, waterslide transfer over gold clay, waterslide transfer over one-half metallic silver and one-half white clay combined, and waterslide transfer over metallic pearl clay.

Metallic powder is rubbed over the clay surface, then stamped with an inked texture plate.

Transfer is applied over treated clay.

mon programs like Microsoft® Word or Photoshop®, even novice computer users can customize the desired image. It only takes seconds to apply to unbaked clay.

Being a fan of ephemera (collectible papers), it also occurred to me that collages of these old tintypes, photos, labels, postcards, and such would be great for creative people to use in making clay jewelry, accessories, and home décor.

Both the blank and preprinted transfer sheets are a translucent film, but the application process differs slightly between the two. Transfers work best on light-colored clays. White clay will offer the most color saturation, allowing the image to stand out visually. Metallic

pearl and light beige clays will give an antiqued appearance to transfers. Placing a transfer image over metallic gold clay can offer the look of an ancient fresco. Transfers applied over a 1:1 mix of metallic silver and white clays resemble the look of paintings on pewter (see the photo on the facing page).

It's also fun to experiment with layering these transfers over foiled clay, crackled metallic leafing, or clay that has been lightly accented with pearlized mica powder, paints, or inks. Consider rubber-stamping inked patterns or text either under or on top of your applied transfers. You can even layer transfers over other transfers.

Transfer is layered over preprinted crackle transfer for an antiqued appearance.

tip

You can create special effects by blurring the edges of the custom inkjet transfers to give a distressed look to your work. Use a damp cotton swab to blur the ink around the edges (or anywhere you like) on the transfer (see below). Do not oversaturate the swab, as it's impossible to control where water will go on the transfer. Blot any excess moisture, and allow the transfer to dry before using.

TECHNIQUE #2

Custom Inkjet Transfers

For pages that contain lettering, the printer needs to be set for reverse printing. This may be listed in the printer dialog menu as "reverse image," "mirror image," or "T-shirt transfer." If you forget to reverse the image, then the letters will appear backward when applying the transfers to polymer clay.

Make sure to allow several minutes for the ink to dry before using the transfers. The pages measure the size of one half-sheet of copy paper. It's most economical to fill an entire page before printing. Once you cut into the page, you will not be able to reprint on any blank areas that remain. Set the size of the document (in whichever program you are using to paste photos or images) to measure 5¼ in. by 8½ in. and then fill the entire area before printing.

When dry, trim the desired transfer to the size and shape required using scissors before application. Once applied, craft knives and clay blades won't cut through the material.

Additional trimming after application should be done with scissors to cut through the transfer and the clay together. Paper punches (often used for scrapbooking) are also a wonderful way to cut your transfers into different sizes and shapes before application.

Place the image facedown over light-colored clay. Starting at one end of the transfer, burnish (rub) the image onto the clay using firm pressure with your index finger. Doing this from one end to the other will force out any trapped air. Clay that isn't completely flat and smooth may also result in air bubbles forming during baking.

Dampen the back of the transfer paper with a few drops of water. When the paper is thoroughly saturated, allow it to sit for 30 to 60 seconds. Blot away any excess water and slide the backing off with your finger. Gently clean the residue from the transfer with a baby wipe or paper towel.

If air bubbles appear between the clay and the transfer, smooth them toward the edges with a dampened fingertip. If this doesn't work, lift up the corner nearest to the bubble and reapply the film to the clay with your fingertip.

Seal the transfer with liquid polymer clay before baking. A very thin layer will leave a matte finish, and a thicker layer will give a satin finish. Unsealed transfers may peel away from clay over time. Bake transfers in a preheated oven according to the manufacturer's directions. Always use an oven thermometer. When finished, transfers can be given a glasslike appearance with one or more layers of Magic-Glos resin.

TECHNIQUE #3

Preprinted Waterslide Transfers

The ink used to print these transfers is waterproof. This is why the images with lettering appear face-forward. Simply saturate the backing of the trimmed transfer with water. Wait 1 to 2 minutes before starting to slide the backing off. Do not slide it off completely or the film will curl into a roll and be hard to control.

Once the backing begins to slide freely, place the exposed end of the film down onto the clay. Burnish the film firmly with one finger while sliding the backing off with your other hand.

Working from one direction to the other while doing this will help eliminate any air bubbles from forming. For best results, seal the transfer with liquid clay as described on the facing page and bake as soon as possible after applying.

Other types of media to use for creating clay transfers include inkjet T-shirt transfer material and clear adhesive inkjet decals.

TECHNIQUE #4

Stamps as Transfers

Using decorative stamps is another method for transferring images onto your clay. It is most easily done using uncured clay. Rubber and silicone stamps vary greatly in the intricacy of designs available. Rubber plates that are similar to photo-etched or pixilated image plates are too detailed for texture work on clay but are great for ink applications (see the photo below).

Liquid Clay Transfers

These types of transfers are popular but can be more difficult to do. This method will require a greater amount of experimentation than other methods of image transfer, but it can be great fun nonetheless.

Because there are three types of liquid clays, each with different properties, including viscosity (thickness) and degrees of clearness, the finished quality can vary considerably. Also, results can be mixed since not all inks and papers will transfer well.

Many people have reported success with transferring images from toner photocopies, inkjet prints, colored/graphite pencil drawings, and laser copies. I recommend that if you achieve a successful transfer using a method, make note of the ink, paper, and printing process used to achieve it for future reference.

Coat the image to be transferred with a layer of liquid clay. You can brush it on in thin layers, allowing it to cure between applications, or you can just pour it onto the image. Thinner layers will be the clearest, but they need to be thick enough that they won't tear easily when removing the paper backing.

The clay can either be baked according to manufacturer's directions or cured with a heat gun. You can visibly see a transformation in the surface of the clay when it is cured using a heat gun. The best way I can describe it is that it almost looks like a skin has formed, like the skin on thick pudding.

Extreme care should be used when handling a heat gun. It emits heat at a much higher temperature than what is recommended for curing liquid clay.

tip

Brushes used for applying liquid clay cannot be washed. They should remain dedicated to liquid clay once they have been used for this purpose.

Wipe the bristles thoroughly after use and store the brush with the handle down. Cover the bristle end with a small plastic bag to protect from accumulation of dust and debris when not in use.

You can modulate this by holding the gun 3 in. to 4 in. away from the clay's surface and moving it continuously while heating.

When baked or heat-gunned clay is completely cool, you may be able to peel the paper off. If this doesn't work, soak the clay in water until the paper is thoroughly saturated. Gently rub away the paper with your finger until all traces of it are gone. This may require resoaking it one or more times. Not all of the image will transfer onto the clay. The finished product will be a somewhat lighter version of the original (see the center photo on the facing page).

Liquid clay transfers are dimensional by nature, but they can be embedded into another clay surface or attached with a layer of liquid clay. Also, keep in mind that these transfers are translucent, thus revealing the underlying color of the clay used.

One cool thing about liquid clay transfers is that they work as window clings (decals) and can be pressed onto smooth glass or metal surfaces as decorations. They are easily removed by simply pulling them off. If they get dirty, rinsing them under water and air-drying them will make them cling once again.

Finished pieces are typically not as crisp and clear as waterslide or toner transfers, but this method can be used when an altered or more rustic outcome is desired (see the right photo on the facing page).

TECHNIQUE #6

Toner-Based Transfers

Perhaps as a child you had the thrill of flattening Silly Putty® over the comics page and seeing a mirror image transferred onto it as you pulled it away. This type of image transfer is akin to toner-based transfers.

This is a very easy method for transferring images onto polymer clay. Toner inks are the ones used for newspapers and photocopies. Toner should not be confused with laser, thermal, or inkjet images. The chemical properties and adhesion to paper differ greatly with these other methods of printing.

Toner inks come in powder form. Black-and-white copies work best for this method. It's helpful to note that, several years back, a technique discovered by Rebecca Krahula using gin as a transfer agent worked quite well for colored toner copies.

In an effort to be more competitive with the growing home inkjet printer market, photocopier manufacturers began to reformulate toner inks to make them less expensive. These changes made the process of transferring colored-toner copies rather hit-or-miss, if not impossible. Although you may have access to a machine that produces color copies that can be transferred to clay using this method, with newer toners, the results tend to be inconsistent. For this reason, this method isn't detailed in this book.

tip

Missing areas in toner transfers can be touched up with a permanent or alcohol ink pen in a matching color.

When working with black-and-white toner copies, it may be helpful to adjust the copier to a slightly darker than normal setting. This will help transfer a clearer, more distinct image. Also, working on white or light-colored clays will give the most crisp and distinct images. But don't be afraid to experiment with colored clays, metallic clays, and gradient backgrounds to create special effects.

Clay, paper, and toner formulas vary greatly. It may take a bit of experimenting on your part to find the combination that gives you the best results.

To create a toner copy, place the copy facedown over well-conditioned clay that's been rolled flat. Any ripples, divots, or lines in the clay's surface will become areas where the copy will not make contact with the clay and will prevent the toner from transferring (see page 69).

Burnish the back of the paper firmly by rubbing vigorously with your finger with some pressure. For best results, allow the copy to sit for some time before placing into a preheated oven. Usually, 5 to 10 minutes will be sufficient. The longer the paper sits on the clay, the darker the transfer tends to be. The paper remains on the clay during the baking process and won't burn.

When the clay has cooled slightly, pull off the paper. The image should be imprinted onto the clay's surface. If the paper sticks, wet it thoroughly and gently roll it off the baked clay until completely removed.

TECHNIQUE #7
Coloring Toner Transfers

There are two options for coloring your toner transfers. The first is to simply color the photocopy with colored pencils. The darker you color the paper, the more intense the color will be in your transfer. Some of the pigment will always remain on the paper, so don't be afraid to use a heavy hand when coloring if you want more saturation.

You can also achieve a softer, tinted effect by coloring the image lightly. Factors such as how long you allow the transfer to sit before baking and how heavy the pencil is applied will all affect the finished appearance of your transfer. As with all creative endeavors, the more you practice, the more control you'll have with the outcome.

Try your hand at working with pastels, chalks, or other mediums to color your photocopy before applying.

Another means of adding color to toner transfers is to color the clay after baking. Keep in mind that, once applied, the medium you use will not be removable. Watercolor and acrylic paints, markers, and inks are mediums to consider for adding color to baked clay.

Deli Paper Transfers

This parchmentlike paper, or "patty paper," as it is sometimes called, is great for making your own custom image transfers. You can draw outlines using a graphite pencil directly on the nonwaxed side of the paper. The heavier the line, the better the images transfer.

Just as with photocopy transfers, you can create, tint, or shade the image using colored pencils. Remember that the image will appear in reverse of what's drawn, so if lettering is used, you should first draw a draft of the image on the waxed side.

Trace the letters or images on the opposite side to reverse them. Bake with the paper in place following the same directions for toner transfers.

Protecting Transfers

The protection of waterslide and stamped-image transfers has already been addressed in this chapter. Since toner and deli paper transfers in high-contact work are subject to wear and tear, too, it's a good idea to protect them by sealing. Applications of liquid clay, compatible resin (Magic-Glos), or glazes (FIMO Gloss Lacquer, Varathane, and Future) are options for sealing transfers. Since some inks or paints may bleed when coming into contact with liquid protectants, make a test sample transfer first to avoid any unpleasant surprises on work that may have taken hours to create.

Aerosol protectants and sealing finishes are not clay compatible. Solvent-based Varathane and clear nail polish are also not recommended. All of these products contain solvents that will react with clay over time, causing the surface to remain tacky indefinitely.

CHAPTER SIX

Mokumé Gané

THIS ADAPTIVE TECHNIQUE is pronounced "mah-ku-may gone-ay." Originally a metalsmithing technique discovered in the 17th century by sword maker Denbei Shoami, the term literally means wood (moku), eye (mé), and metal (gan). It is also often translated as "wood grain metal." Shoami's artistic discovery was the result of a serendipitous accident. His original intention was to find a way to strengthen swords by layering various types of metals. He discovered that when these layered metals were cut against the grain, various intricate patterns emerged.

Polymer clay is an ideal medium for achieving unique, pleasing patterns for surface decoration based on the original Mokumé Gané concept. Being easier to work with than metal, polymer clay offers many more options for manipulation than metal in creating a wide variety of effects.

There are several variations, some yet to be discovered, that can be applied in creating Mokumé Gané treatments. Basically, the technique involves creating stacked sheets or loaves of layered, rolled, or folded clays. The clay is then manipulated or distorted by piercing, cutting, or pressing with tools or textures.

TECHNIQUES

- Stamped Mokumé Gané
- Bladed Mokumé Gané
- Indented Mokumé Gané
- Folded Mokumé Gané
- Rolled Mokumé Gané

This versatile concept can also incorporate inclusions such as metal leafing, foils, inks, acrylic paint, or embossing powders. Various means of manipulation can also be combined when creating the loaves or layered stacks that make up a Mokumé Gané block. Once created, thin slices are shaved off the block and typically rolled into a clay base until the two levels are melded seamlessly.

Results can range from very abstract to pattern-specific depending on the methods used when making Mokumé Gané. Regardless of the outcome, the results are generally aesthetically pleasing and easy to achieve. This technique is ideal for beginners since the outcome often appears more complex and difficult than it actually is.

Mokumé Gané is a wonderful surface treatment for the creation of more masculine gifts, especially when deep, dark tones or metallic clays are used.

Many find experimentation with the technique very satisfying. Try your hand at using translucent clays with opaque ones. Also, consider the use of found objects when manipulating clay. Color combinations, whether bold or subtle, usually yield pleasing outcomes.

Again, as with most of the areas covered in this book, it would be entirely possible to write a book solely devoted to variations of this technique. I have offered just a handful of possibilities to tempt you. Mokumé Gané is one of the most user-friendly techniques for polymer clay and a great place to start if you're new to the medium.

TECHNIQUE #1
Stamped Mokumé Gané

1 Select three colors of clay that complement one another, yet have some contrast. After conditioning all the clays from lightest to darkest, roll out each color on the fourth-largest setting of the pasta machine.

2 Trim each sheet to 4 in. by 4 in. and stack one over the other in an order that alternates colors to create the most contrast.

3 Roll the stack through the largest setting of the pasta machine and cut it into quarters.

4 Stack these pieces, one over the other, so that the colors continue to alternate. This will create a striped loaf.

5 Press the loaf down firmly over a deeply detailed texture stamp. This will compress the layers and form internal patterns.

tip

Flexible clay blades work best for shaving. Blades should be clean and sharp. Bending the blade into an arc may be helpful when making shavings.

6 Shave very thin layers from the textured clay loaf using the clay blade. Press these first shavings onto the underside of the loaf.

Detailed patterns usually don't appear until you've repeated Step 5 two or more times. Continue repeating the instructions in Step 5 until interesting patterns emerge.

7 Place the slices face up and randomly over a layer of a fourth color of clay for the background color. Roll the slices into the background using an acrylic roller until they are melded together seamlessly.

tip

Examine the slices from both sides to determine which patterns are more appealing.

Cut these sheets into shapes for jewelry or apply larger sheets onto bakeable surfaces. Mokumé Gané slices are also beautiful over beads formed from unbaked clay.

VARIATION

The above method will result in random patterns. For more specific patterns using stamps, make a clay sheet (as opposed to a larger loaf) from thinly rolled layers of three or four stacked colors of clay. Impress the sheet very firmly so that it is deeply embossed. This will only be done once as opposed to the random-effect method described previously.

Shave off the raised areas of the pattern to reveal the pattern below. Try to shave as closely as possible to the lower recesses formed when stamping without shaving too deeply, or you will lose the patterning. If any slightly raised areas remain, they can be smoothed flat with the roller (see the top right photo). Be sure to save the more interesting shavings for rolling onto another clay background (see photo at right).

Polishing Mokumé Gané surfaces after baking (following instructions beginning in chapter 1, page 19) can give a rich and elegant finish to your work. Polishing can also create an illusion of depth in your patterns. Extreme sanding with lower grits of sandpaper before working up to finer grits, and buffing can actually alter the pattern by revealing variations that didn't appear on the surface after baking. This is just one more concept to play with on your creative journey!

> **tip**
> With continued work, the loaf will not only get thinner but it will also flatten and spread. When this occurs, you can cut the loaf in half and restack to give greater height to the clay for slicing.

TECHNIQUE #2

Bladed Mokumé Gané

1 Another method of getting interesting grains and patterns in your Mokumé Gané is one I learned from Trudy Schwartz-Burrill. Roll out three to four colors of clay on the third- or fourth-largest setting of the pasta machine. Rather than stacking layer over layer, tear the clay sheets and assemble them randomly into a loaf. While this method can work with any type of patterning for Mokumé Gané, it's especially beautiful when cutting the loaf repeatedly with a straight or wavy clay blade.

2 Press the dull edge of your blade into the torn clay loaf several times, making straight or diagonal slices almost to the other side of the loaf without cutting all the way through. Recompress the sliced loaf with your hands so the slices are melded back together. Flip the loaf over and repeat.

3 Do this 5 to 10 more times on each side of the loaf and compress the clay back together every time. The more you repeat this process, the more complex the resulting pattern will be.

Typically, you would cut thin slices from across the top of the loaf as opposed to shavings (as with stamped Mokumé Gané) for use in your creations. To create a larger surface area, adjoin several slices together over a base layer of clay that won't show.

White clay is best for abutting these slices together since it won't dull or muddy the color, because the clays will thin from rolling. Use the acrylic roller first to meld seams together, and then finish with the pasta machine to create a flat, smooth, and integrated sheet.

VARIATION

Using thicker tools, such as the edge of an old plastic hotel key or expired credit card, will yield more pronounced veining.

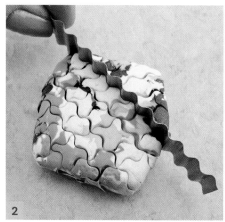

Indented Mokumé Gané

Impressing a stacked or torn Mokumé Gané loaf using tools or found objects can be a lot of fun. Some objects that are ideal for this include knitting needles of various dimensions, metal pipes that will leave ring patterns, and spindles from the center of adding machine tapes. Think of objects that have deep and detailed crevices that will incise a pattern into the layers of your loaf.

Another creative option is to shave layers from indented areas and apply them to a base-clay layer of a different color (as with stamped Mokumé Gané). This technique is wide open in terms of the fun you can have exploring it, so try everything!

VARIATION

In indented loaves that have open holes, roll snakes of contrasting or translucent clays and press them in to fill these openings. Cutting thin slices from a back-filled loaf (as with bladed Mokumé Gané) works best when utilizing this method, as does slicing shavings from indented loaves with open holes.

tip

As you repeatedly slice the loaf, the holes will become smaller and smaller toward the bottom. When this happens, widen these using the same tools you employed to make the holes.

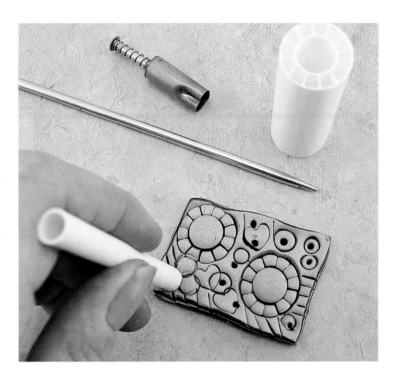

TECHNIQUE #4
Folded Mokumé Gané

Create a layered sheet of clay as described in | STAMPED MOKUMÉ GANÉ, page 74 |. Fold this sheet several times in any way you prefer until a small, compact loaf is formed. Try rolling the layered sheet more thinly to make folding easier. You'll see (below) that the result is a more detailed pattern.

Next, try applying clay foil or metallic leafing on several or all of the clay layers before stacking. You'll see this can create striking effects.

TECHNIQUE #5
Rolled Mokumé Gané

Yet another beautiful alternative is to roll layered sheets of clay like a jelly roll. Slices are cut from the roll at an angle to reveal sections that look much like the core of a tree. This method is especially lovely when created with alternating layers of translucent clay, or translucent clay sandwiched with layers of foil or leaf (see the top left photo on the facing page).

Stack very thin slices over a base layer of clay. The thinner the clay, the more the underlying color will come through, especially after polishing (see the bottom photo on the facing page). Play with overlapping rolled slices as you embed them into the base layer with a roller for intersecting patterns. For your background clay consider using | BASIC SKINNER BLENDING sheets, chapter 3, page 39 |.

The multitude of options and varieties that can be achieved with a single concept like Mokumé Gané are enough to boggle the mind! Have fun and try as many as you can. See my website, www.lisapavelka.com, for more artwork inspiration.

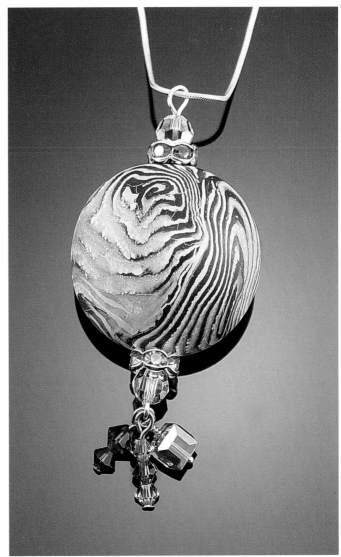

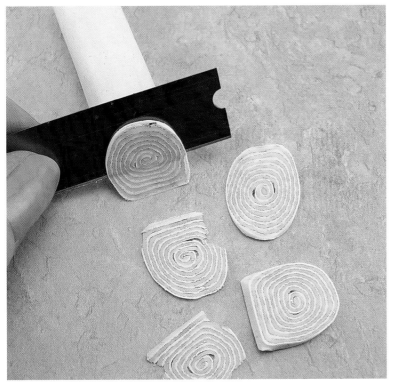

Very thin strips of translucent clay are covered with foil and leaf on both sides, then layered over a very thin sheet of white clay before rolling.

The roll is sliced diagonally to reveal ringed layers of clay and metallic specks. The thinner the slices, the better when layering over base clay.

CHAPTER SEVEN

Mica Shift Effects

AMONG THE MANY IMITATIVE QUALITIES of polymer clay, metallic effects are some of the easiest, yet most dramatic to achieve. These effects can create the illusion of solid minerals or metals or just add a touch of metallic color or shimmer.

Mica-embedded polymer clay offers a technique called Mica Shift that is unique to the medium, not to be duplicated by any other material. In this chapter, we'll explore a handful of materials and basic techniques that will create stunning visual surface treatments to use in your artwork.

TECHNIQUES

- Mica Shift Surface and Border Treatments
- Mica Shift Checkerboard Cane
- Embossed Mica Shifting
- Mosaic Mica Shifting
- Wood Grain Mica Shifting

What Is Mica Shift?

This is a manipulation technique that can be done only with mica-based metallic polymer clays. Clay that is labeled "metallic" by virtue of glitter inclusions is not the metallic clay we are referring to for this technique. The overall effect is typically considered to have a holographic effect or the illusion of wood grain.

Like many happy accidents that led to new clay techniques, there were serendipitous discoveries that led to Mica Shift techniques. It was learned that metallic clays reveal a shadowed cross grain when sliced or conditioned. When you slice into a block of metallic gold clay, for instance, you can see that the top surface appears lighter than the sliced side. It's almost as

if they are actually two different shades of the same color.

It was this property that led polymer clay pioneers Pier Voulkos and Mike Buesseler to further explore and develop methods for creating patterns with these types of clay. We'll look at two basic means of working with this unique property to create patterns in the surface of the clay: Stamped/Embossed and Rolled/ Stacked Mica Shifting.

CHATOYANCY

What causes this effect is the chatoyant nature of the embedded mica particles. *Chatoyancy* is a word with French origins meaning "cat's eye" (*chat* for "cat" and *oeil* for "eye"). It is a scientific reference to the optical reflective properties of animal eyes seen from certain angles at night and in the fibrous structure of certain stones such as chrysoberyl and tiger eye. If you were born before CDs replaced record albums, you may remember twisting and turning records in your hands to see the hourglass-shaped light that seemed to rotate around the disk. This too is an example of chatoyancy.

Essentially, millions of nearly microscopic particles act as tiny mirrors that reflect light in different directions. By controlling the direction these little mirror-like particles lie, one can create surface contrasts of clay against clay that reveal patterns not limited to but including concentric swirls, checkerboards, stripes, ribbons, and wood-grain illusions.

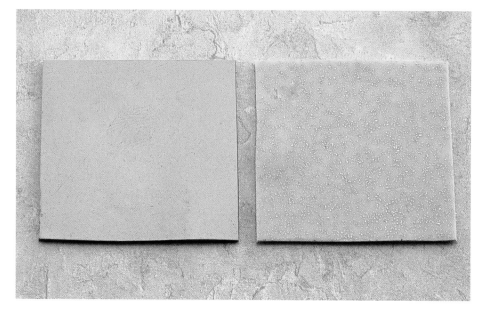

Slice into any block of unconditioned metallic clay, and you'll most likely reveal what appears to be clay with lines of different color inside, or a "grain." These are the tiny particles facing in different directions.

The first method of Mica Shifting evolved through the discoveries of artist Voulkos, who refers to the manipulation of metallic clays as "invisible caning."

Artist Judy Belcher calls this concept "caning in one color." The results can be more subtle and organic than Stamped/Embossed Mica Shifting. There are dozens of manipulations that include stacking, cutting, twisting, or folding the clay after conditioning to get various specific and random patterns. We'll learn one of these patterns in this chapter.

METALLIC CLAY OPTIONS

These clays are available among several of the commonly found brands of clay. The number of colors available varies from brand to brand, but all of the clays found with this property are available in a minimum of metallic colors, including pearl white, gold, silver, and copper shades.

Pearl clay may be combined with other nonmetallic clay colors to create new shades and colors of metallic clay. For best results, 50 percent or more metallic clay should be included with any color blend.

Regardless of the type of Mica Shifting you are doing, it is essential to condition the clay in a way that causes all the mica particles to face the same direction. This is done through pasta machine conditioning. Continually roll the metallic clay you are working with through the largest setting until you get a sheet with a smooth surface appearance. Always fold the sheet in half and insert it in the same direction with each pass until there are no visible striations on the surface area. (This cannot be avoided around the edges.) Now you have a sheet that is ready to form.

Mica Shift Surface and Border Treatments

It's easy to make Mica Shift border treatments by cutting strips of conditioned metallic clay and twisting or rolling them to create dual-shaded effects with a single color of clay.

RIBBONS

You can control the thickness and width of strips you twist.

1 Stacking multiple conditioned sheets, one over the other, can make wider strips. Be sure to compress the layers well with an acrylic rod.

2 Also consider the type of project you are creating when determining the thickness of each of the strips you are slicing. Twisting the strips will create an elegant effect along the edges of many types of projects.

3 Control the space between stripes by starting to twist at one end and moving your fingers down the length as you continue.

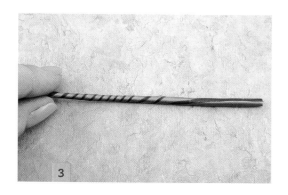

STRIPED SNAKES

1 For rolled or rounded edging, cut strips of clay from conditioned sheets or loaves that are as wide as they are tall. Round the corner edges on all four sides by compressing them with your fingers.

2 When the strip is somewhat rounded, roll the strip to a snake of the desired diameter and twist. The dually shaded lines may appear to be distorted, but this will disappear when you twist the snake.

3 As with the twisting of thinner strips, begin at one end and work your way down, little by little, to control the distance between stripes.

PATTERNED OVERLAYS

Create a variety of surface treatments by cutting strips or shapes from thin sheets cut with the "cross grain" from a conditioned metallic loaf.

1 The pieces should be laid face up (with the darker side showing). Cut sections with blades or cutters and apply to a conditioned sheet of the same metallic clay.

2 Roll the overlays into the clay until they are seamlessly embedded.

This method allows complete control over creating all types of patterns. You can roll very thin striped Mica Shift snakes to create these patterns or even form letters that appear to glow when blended into the clay background.

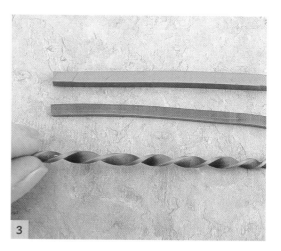

Mica Shift
Checkerboard Cane

This is just one of the many types of invisible canes you can create using only a single color of metallic clay.

1 Condition a 2-oz. block of metallic clay. Cut away the edges to create a uniform square sheet.

2 Cut this sheet into equal quarters and stack, compressing the loaf with your acrylic rod. If necessary, condition more clay and roll it through the thickest setting on your pasta machine to make more squares to build the stack into slices of equal thickness (⅛ in. is a good thickness). You'll need an even number of slices. Leave them lying in the order in which they were sliced.

3 Assemble the slices, rotating every other slice a quarter turn so that the reassembled loaf appears to be striped. The darker strip is a view of the cross grain in the clay.

4 Turn the stack and slice again through the loaf, cutting slices of the same thickness as in the previous step. Reassemble the slices by turning every other one 180 degrees (upside down).

The slices in this step break down each strip into small squares. When reassembled with the darker and lighter squares alternating, you'll have created a checkerboard pattern. It's important to make slices as uniform as possible when doing this project in order to get the tightest alignment. Lightly compress the cane with your hand or a roller **a**.

Slices from the cane can be abutted against one another with checks alternating to create large surface areas with this treatment **b**.

2

4a

4b

Embossed Mica Shifting

This method of manipulating metallic clays can be done using deep-relief rubber stamps, textures, and a variety of tools. The idea is to create patterns by compressing the clay's surface and shaving off the uppermost layer to reveal a ghosted image beneath.

To better explain how and why this technique works, you can think of it as a manner of bruising the clay. When firm pressure is applied to a sheet of thick to medium-thick conditioned metallic clay, the mica particles are tightly compacted together. When the raised layer of the clay is completely shaved off, the compressed patterns are revealed. The technique itself is very easy, but it takes some practice to get good results. This is not a method to rush through. Patience is your ally here. If you practice this a bit, you'll find that it can be a very Zen-like technique and quite relaxing.

It's best to work with thicker slices of clay to ensure that there is enough depth to get a detailed impression of the texture. The clay will be thinned both through the shaving and rolling process in later steps.

I generally use sheets rolled on the thickest setting of the pasta machine, but when a thinner finished sheet is needed, it's okay to roll the clay thinner before embossing as long as there is enough depth to get a detailed, raised pattern (see the top photo at left).

Always use a clean, sharp clay blade. Flexible blades work best. Carefully wipe the blade frequently to remove stray particles of clay (see the bottom photo at left).

Set the shavings off to one side of your work area to make sure they are not picked up and redeposited onto the clay sheet.

Don't try to shave off too much clay in one pass. Small, thin slices work best. You may have to shave the same area more than once until no more raised impressions remain.

Bending the blade is helpful in giving you control over the blade.

Do not shave too deeply, as the ghosted impression is quite shallow.

When you think you're done, look at your sheet from all angles to make sure all raised areas have been shaved off. If any raised areas remain, they will show up as hairline cracks after the clay is flattened and smoothed with your roller or pasta machine.

These aren't actual cracks and won't affect the structural integrity of the clay. They are just the edges of raised clay that weren't shaved enough, folding down onto the sheet. The edges will flatten to reveal a thin cross-grain side, which appears as a crack.

Polishing Mica Shifted clay or covering it with a thick layer of UV resin after baking will deepen the holographic quality of the pattern by causing the surface to appear more dimensional. It's quite fun to see the shock on someone's face when they touch the satiny smooth surface of Mica Shifted clay and realize what they thought was a texture is, in fact, a flat one.

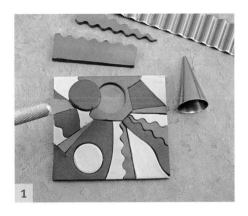

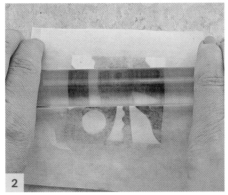

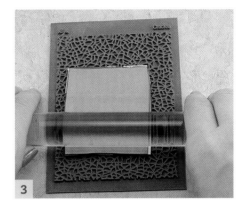

TECHNIQUE #4
Mosaic Mica Shifting

Combine multiple metallic-colored clays into a convergent Mica Shifted design by deeply stamping two or more different colored and conditioned mica clay sheets using the identical texture or stamp. Once the desired number of metallic-colored clays have been prepared and rolled through a larger pasta machine setting, follow these steps.

1 Components of your design can be in the form of stripes, freehand interlocking shapes, or pieces cut from a pattern drawn onto card stock.

Assemble the pieces of your design over a thin sheet of light-colored clay. The pieces should be abutted against one another as closely as possible for the tightest fit.

2 Place deli or parchment paper over the clay and roll firmly with an acrylic rod until all the pieces meld together seamlessly. It's helpful to rotate the clay assembly as you do this step to make sure the clay stretches uniformly.

3 Lay the sheet face down over the texture of your choice and emboss with one firm pass with the roller. Shave the raised clay, working with small sections at a time, and then flatten | see EMBOSSED MICA SHIFTING on the facing page |.

These sheets make beautiful surface treatments for many projects, such as the evening bag seen here (at right). The more colors of mica-based clay you use in your design, the more finished "mosaic" sheets you can assemble with the pieces (two colors will allow you to create two veneers, three colors will allow for making three veneer sheets, and so on).

TECHNIQUE #5

Wood-Grain Mica Shifting

With all this talk of cross grain, wood-work may have come to mind. Creating wood illusions with Mica Shifting concepts is yet another amazing manipulation of metallic clays. While it is a faux technique, it also is best addressed in this chapter.

Clay artist Robert Wiley has perfectly mimicked the look of parquetry, marquetry, and intarsia using Mica Shifted clay in his creations (for a look at his work, see page 200 of the Gallery). These are all methods for tightly assembling different types of wood to create geometric and pictorial patterns. This art form has been used for many hundreds of years in the creation of flooring and decorative veneers for furniture, accessories, and walls.

Mixing small amounts of various colors (such as reds and browns) with gold and copper metallic clays can create shades that mimic the shades of various stained woods.

1 Create several (three to four) colors of wood-tone shades of mica-based clay. The samples here were made using the following ratios of clay (from lightest to darkest):

- 1:1 of Metallic Gold
  mixed with Metallic Pearl

- 1:1 of Metallic Gold
  mixed with Metallic Copper

- 2:1 of Metallic Copper
  mixed with Caramel

2 After thoroughly mixing the clay, fold it into a larger ball, making sure to compress air out as you do. Chop the lump of clay into several pieces and mix these up. Recompress the pieces into a single ball of clay. After tightly compacting it, roll the clay into a snake.

3 Twist the ends of the snake 6 to 8 times. Compress the ends in on themselves and twist some more until fine, darker lines appear across the entire length of the snake. Recompress the snake to a shorter length and twist several more times to create even finer lines.

4 Compress the snake into a shorter length with your hands until it is a few inches across and thicker.

5 Flatten the snake a bit by hand and then roll it through the pasta machine through several settings to create thin, woodlike sheets. Use these to create faux wood effects like the tumbling blocks pattern seen below. The type of finish, whether satin or glossy, depends on your personal preference.

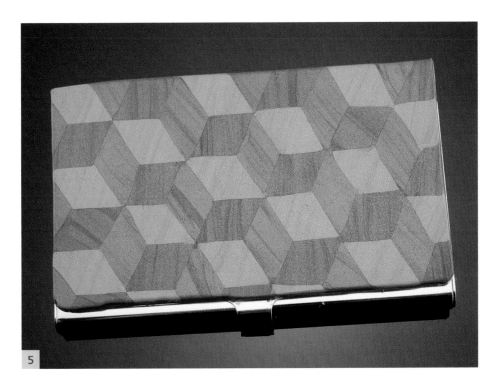

...since I watched you sail.

...ths of my love for you my own.

...easy and they fail to flo...

...could I can only try to...

...heart for you to try and und...

...was a lonely and barren wa...

...d on my horizon. I pass the ho...

CHAPTER EIGHT

Leaf and Foiling Effects

MYLAR-BACKED FOILS AND METAL LEAFING are versatile materials that offer a large number of effects for polymer clay surfaces and inclusions. These two products are similar, as they both create a metallic finish with clay, but the applications and results can be quite different.

Mylar-backed foils come in many more colors than leafing. They are heat-sensitive products that can be applied to polymer clay and other creative surfaces through adhesives. Foils also come in a variety of patterns and effects. Both foils and leafing are very economical, as a little goes a long way, and there is no wasted product if it's properly handled and stored. How much leafing or foil you use will typically be determined by the desired finish or color you are looking to achieve.

TECHNIQUES

- Metal Leafing
- Polymer Clay Foil
- Applying Foil
- Foil Textures and Dimensions
- Foil Pattern Resists
- The Pavelka Peel

Metal Leafing

Metal leafing comes in two basic forms: precious metal leaf, which can be 24-karat gold, and other precious metals or composition leaf, which is made up of alloys to resemble gold and silver leafing. Copper leaf is typically genuine copper. It's important to note that if left untreated or unsealed, gold and copper leaf will darken with time.

Composition silver leaf is made from aluminum and will not darken or tarnish. For our purposes, I will always refer to composition metal leafing since this type of leaf is what I recommend for polymer clay work. It costs a fraction of what a precious metal leaf does.

Metal leafing typically comes in packages of 25 sheets layered between tissue paper or in flakes. There are variations of heat-treated leafing that give rainbow effects and colorcasts of gold and red. Copper leaf can be treated with a heat gun to create similar color variations.

In order to prevent burning your clay, heat treatments should be done before applying metal leafing to polymer clay, as a heat gun can reach temperatures in excess of those recommended for curing clay.

Its almost-lighter-than-air consistency makes working with leaf a bit challenging. Make sure your hands are clean and dry before handling it. This product is extremely fragile and can either be cut with scissors or torn. Using scissors is the best way to control the size and amount of leaf you want to use.

Leaf adheres easily to uncured polymer clay. In addition to the possibility of some forms of leafing tarnishing over time, all leaf can be worn away by handling after baking. To preserve color or surface treatment, sealing is recommended.

Depending on the finished look you like, you may want to seal leafing with liquid clay for an invisible, matte, or satiny appearance. UV resin can also be applied after baking. When using liquid clay, it's best to heat-set the leafed clay for 5 to 10 minutes first. When the clay has cooled, apply liquid clay with a

Silver leaf on black clay (left). Silver foil on black clay (right). Both pieces have been stretched through four settings of a pasta machine.

brush or your finger. Attempting to apply liquid clay before heat setting can cause the leaf to flake off on your brush or fingers.

Leaf not only handles differently than clay foil, but it responds differently to stretching. Leaf will crackle much more easily when stretched or thinned. The result is much more dramatic than it is with foiled clay, as can be seen in the samples in the top photos on the facing page.

Polymer Clay Foil

My love of foiled clay work began in the mid-1990s, when I happened to get samples of Mylar-backed foils for imprinting. I was delighted to find that some of these would adhere to uncured clay. Once I started playing, I couldn't stop. Necessity led me to search for foils that would work consistently on polymer clay and to make these available for other creative people.

I currently offer more than a dozen colors and patterns of Mylar-backed foil specifically made for clay and crafting use. To this day, using foils in my polymer clay work is still a favorite endeavor.

Being a huge fan of dichroic glass artwork and jewelry, I immediately recognized the similarities between foiled clay and the more costly and labor-intensive medium of dichroic glass. My earliest attempts to duplicate the look of dichroic glass exceeded my wildest hopes when experts at a glass exposition mistakenly assumed the beads on my badge holder were dichroic glass.

The very first results were achieved using the relatively new medium of liquid clay. This product helped simulate the depth found in a lot of dichroic work and allowed me to polish the clay without removing the foil. Unfortunately, when I tried thicker applications of liquid clay, the clarity was reduced, as was the realistic depth found in many types of dichroic work.

Frustration over this limitation led me to work on a dimensional glazing product for clay that would allow the creation of greater depth and clarity. Limitations for this product led to the further development of Magic-Glos UV resin for polymer clay. With this resin, it's easy to achieve eye-fooling dichroic and glass art effects that include dimensional effects, layered foil, and patterns that cannot be achieved with traditional dichroic glass work.

Not all Mylar-backed foils work with polymer clay. Some will not adhere, no matter how much you work to apply them. Others will stick in small amounts. Be sure to work with foil that is specifically recommended for polymer clay.

Foils are generally brighter in metallic sheen than leaf and come in many more colors and effects. There are several applications that can be done with foil that cannot be done with leafing. Conversely, clay foil doesn't crackle as noticeably as leaf does. The effect is much more subtle and can dull the intensity of the overall color and finish when stretched.

Different brands and consistencies of polymer clay can make applying foil a bit difficult. Clays with a softer consistency or stickier surfaces typically are easier to apply foil to.

Applying Foil

Foil, even under the best of clay conditions, rarely comes off the Mylar backing completely. Applications to smaller surface areas usually yield the best results. Even then, small pieces of foil may remain on the Mylar. In most instances, these are tiny little specks that, in cases such as stamp embossing and molding, will not even be noticeable. When the foil doesn't adhere to large patches of clay, it can usually be fixed easily.

1 Begin with well-conditioned clay. The clay should be as smooth and flat as possible. Any surface deviation, such as ridges from a pasta machine or divots, can prevent the foil from adhering in spots.

Not all pasta machines create these roll ridges, but it's best to even out the surface with an acrylic rod before applying the foil. Make sure the rod is clean

tip
If you have very cold fingers, warm them first by briskly rubbing them back and forth against your pants leg.

of debris, as anything sticking to it will create a divot in the clay's surface when you roll.

2 Lay the foil with the color facing up toward you. (Pearlidescent is my translucent water-slick-effect foil. The colors appear on both sides of this particular variety. The matte surface is applied directly against the clay so the shiny surface of the pattern faces upward.)

Smooth the foil down from one end toward the other. Use a small piece of deli or scrap paper between your fingertip and the foil to vigorously burnish the entire surface for 30 to 60 seconds.

Remember that the heat of burnishing is what causes the foil to stick to the clay and not pressure. Applying too much pressure can cause surface deviations in your clay. It's important to use the paper

tip
Another thing that can make it hard to get foil to adhere is working with under-conditioned clay or a brand of clay that is very firm.

If you are sure the clay has been properly conditioned, but it still feels very stiff, rub a very tiny amount of liquid clay into the surface. It's important to wipe away as much of the residue as possible in order for the foil to adhere. Apply the foil as described in Step 2.

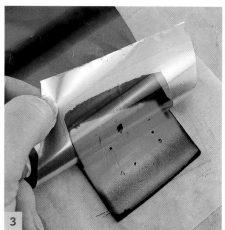

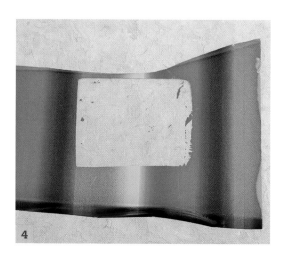

when burnishing since the body oils in your finger will cause drag, which will prevent sufficient friction. Not enough friction means not enough heat and less chance that the foil will release well.

3 Immediately after burnishing, lift a corner of the Mylar backing and pull it backward (not upward) in a ripping motion as quickly as possible. It's very similar to the method used in hair waxing—the faster you pull, the better the results will be. Pulling upward instead of backward will also inhibit the foil from releasing from the backing.

Finally, it's important to pay attention to which corner you pulled the Mylar from if you need to do any patching (as explained in the next step).

4 It's not uncommon to see tiny specks of foil remaining on the Mylar backing. This is typical even when the best application method is followed. These small areas where the foil doesn't adhere are seldom noticeable, especially when using foiled clay for molding or stamped embossing purposes. If larger patches of clay remain

uncovered, this can easily be fixed in most cases, except where there are surface depressions or divots in the clay.

To patch larger spots where the foil didn't stick, simply re-lay the Mylar backing over the clay so that the exposed areas are recovered. This is much like putting the pieces of a puzzle in place. Reburnish (as in step 2), making sure to concentrate heat and pressure while you burnish over the areas where the foil didn't stick.

When you rip the Mylar off for the second time, pull it in a direction different from the one used in the first application. Ripping from a different direction will lay the foil down into exposed spots most of the time, if properly positioned and burnished.

If the area still remains exposed, try burnishing the foil into the spot using a fresh section from an edge or corner. Again, if the foil doesn't stick during this step, it's usually due to a depression in the surface.

Polymer clay foil, like leaf, can wear away with repeated handling or contact.

Protect it with a coat of liquid clay, polymer-clay-compatible sealer, or UV resin. Again, as with leaf, heat-set the clay for a few minutes first before applying liquid clay to prevent it from coming off on your brush or finger.

5 If you find your clay is no longer flat on the surface after applying the foil, place a deli sheet over the top and lightly roll with the acrylic rod. Running the clay through the pasta machine can also be done, but keep in mind that if the setting is much thinner than the clay, the foil may stretch enough to dilute the color or even crackle.

Foil Applications

There are myriad applications for foil with your clay work, many more than can be covered in a single chapter. We'll look at some other types of uses for foil and clay in later chapters, but here is a sampling of exciting applications and tips to get you started.

Foil Textures and Dimensions

Adding surface patterns or shaping your foiled clay can yield amazing results. Leafed clay can also be stamped, molded, and textured, but because of the tendency to crack drastically, a completely different effect is achieved than when the same treatment is done to foiled clay.

Foil typically acts as its own release agent when used with rubber stamps, texture plates, and molds. However, minute flecks of foil may adhere to these surfaces. These are easily wiped or washed away in most cases, but a cleaner release can be achieved if a release agent, such as automotive protectant spray, is used (as discussed in chapter 2). Also, the intensity of the foil will be greater when a release agent is used.

Spraying the release agent directly on a stamp, texture plate, or mold can produce inconsistent results. For the best results in releasing clay, spray a small amount directly onto the foiled clay and spread with your finger. This will ensure that the release agent hits all the crevices of the stamp or mold for a cleaner separation. This will not affect the foil, clay, or stamp/mold.

Foil Pattern Resists

Both versions of this technique were discovered through personal experimentation. The first method I found for creating detailed foil patterns for clay was the result of working with rubber stamps, adhesive embossing powder, and foils for paper crafts.

If you're not familiar with embossing powders, these are thermographic materials that are commonly used in the printing industry to create the shiny, raised text that is often found on business cards and printed invitations. This is done by a mechanized application of colored powders in letter patterns. When the powder is heated, it melts, creating the raised image.

This material has become popular in the crafting world with rubber stamp use. A variety of embossing powders can be found with different finishes, but there will be more on these later. The powder that is used to create one type of pattern resist is a tacky embossing compound that is designed for foil application. A traditional embossing pad is used to stamp a design onto paper.

The ink from these pads is either clear or lightly tinted and is designed to remain wet for several minutes. When you are using it, though, it's best to work as speedily as possible.

1 When the pattern is stamped, quickly pour tacky embossing powder over the inked area. Make sure the powder has a

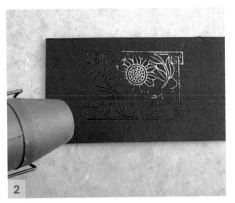

chance to make contact with the entire pattern. Shake off the excess powder onto a tray or over paper and return it to the jar.

2 Heat the embossing powder until just melted. Do not overheat, as this will burn the adhesive. Apply the foil right away, with the color facing up. Burnish firmly with a bone folder.

3 When the foil is cool, quickly rip it off in the same manner used with polymer clay. This will leave a negative version of the pattern on the Mylar backing. This foil can then be burnished onto uncured polymer clay.

Consider the color of clay you are applying the foil pattern to. Colors that offer the most contrast will highlight the pattern best. This is a nifty way to create a matching greeting to accompany a clay gift you create. The recipient will be amazed at how you created mirrored, metallic finishes to your artwork and greeting.

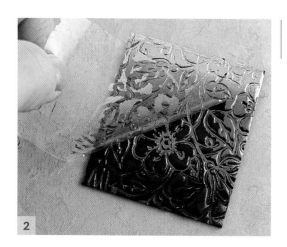

2

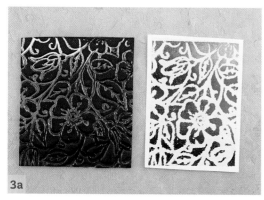

3a

TECHNIQUE #4
The Pavelka Peel

The next method for pattern resist was discovered when I attempted an easier way to create foil patterns on clay several years ago. After stamping foiled clay with a detailed texture plate, I wanted to see what would happen if packing tape was applied to the clay surface and peeled away. *Voila!* The foil remained in the recessed areas, but came off the uppermost surface. Upon showing this to a friend, she immediately dubbed the technique the "Pavelka Peel." Here are some tips for creating detailed and abstract patterns in the surface of clay using this method.

1 Do not apply automotive protectant spray or any other release agent to foiled clay before stamping or texturing for this technique, as it will prevent the tape from removing the foil.

2 After embossing foiled clay, apply the adhesive tape to the surface and lightly burnish with the flat edge of your index finger. Peel the tape off and reveal the inlaid pattern. Applying and burnishing a second application of tape will give a crisper, cleaner finish for this effect. Or, you may prefer the slightly rough edges of the pattern that are left with a single tape application. You be the judge!

3 The tape will now have a reverse image of your pattern foiled onto the back. Save this for application onto other surfaces like paper, for use in making greetings, tags, or other accessories. (The sample on the right is the leftover tape applied to white cardstock after being peeled away from the embossed/foiled clay **a**.)

This is yet another wonderful opportunity to create an additional project, as with the embossing powder method. You've got to love it when waste material can be repurposed for another creative use **b**.

4 Consider how thick your clay should be rolled out before applying the foil. This is determined by how deeply you plan on embossing the foiled clay. You may wish to have a distinctively raised surface apparent in the clay. A deeply embossed area will make it easier to remove foil from the surface without accidentally removing it from the embossed pattern.

5 To create a flat, one-dimensional foil pattern, a more shallow impression must be made. Extreme care and a lighter touch should be used when burnishing the tape over shallow impressions to prevent removing foil in your design.

When the foil has been removed, place deli paper over the clay and roll with an acrylic rod until the surface is completely flat. This will give the surface a look similar to screen printing.

The less surface texture you can apply while still being able to remove only the top layer of foil, the better the pattern will appear when completely flattened. A little practice will go a long way to perfecting the delicate balance between depth and foil removal.

The photo at left below shows (from left to right) stamp-embossed foiled clay, Pavelka Peeled foiled clay, and flattened peeled clay.

6 Create random or abstract patterns by embossing foiled clay with nontraditional materials and tools, including crumpled aluminum foil, found textures, and tools of every shape and size.

This sample was made by pressing the edge of a credit card into gold-covered black clay and removing the surface foil with adhesive tape.

Applying the leftover tape from Pavelka Peeled clay to black card stock made the leafy copper background on this tag.

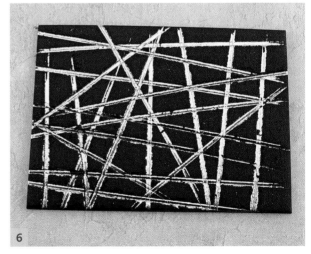

CHAPTER NINE

Faux Effects

FAUX (PRONOUNCED FŌ) IS A FRENCH WORD meaning "false." Whenever *faux* is used with a creative concept, it refers to an imitative effect. Polymer clay is unique in that, perhaps more than any other medium, it can be used to create realistic imitations of almost every material known. The one exception is something crystal clear, such as glass or a faceted gemstone.

This ability makes polymer clay one of the most exciting materials to work with. Few things are more creatively satisfying than having someone mistake an object you made for the material you were attempting to recreate.

You may even be encouraged to tackle your own method for creating the look of a material that no one else has tried. There are numerous "recipes" for some of the techniques contained within this chapter. Regardless of the method you use, all that matters is that the end result closely approximates the look you are hoping to achieve.

Since naturally occurring variations of the materials tackled in this chapter come in a wide array of colors and finishes, tweaking these or other formulas often results in a variation that still offers a realistic approximation of the real thing. The ability to fool the beholder often lies as much in the quality of your finishes as it does the formula itself.

Because some of the faux concepts for clay are so extensive, other chapters touch on additional imitative techniques where applicable, such as Faux Dichroic and Mica Shift wood illusions. Books such as *Polymer: The Chameleon Clay* by Victoria Hughes are exclusively devoted to faux concepts.

TECHNIQUES

- Faux Opal
- Faux Turquoise
- Faux Raku
- Faux Ivory
- Faux Cinnabar
- Faux Rust

Keep in mind that the colors specified for the following formulas are from the FIMO Soft color palette. Since color palettes vary significantly from brand to brand, duplicating these formulas with other brands may require a bit of modification. I hope you enjoy trying your hand at the faux techniques that follow, some of my favorites.

Faux Opal

Opal is a naturally occurring mineraloid gel that offers more color variations than just about any other precious gemstone found on the planet. Opal is Australia's national gemstone, but the material is also found in North America and in fossilized formations. It is known for its fiery and iridescent properties.

Opal often strikingly resembles dichroic glass variations. It's prized for the way it plays with light and seems to glow from within. This recipe for opal is amazingly simple to create.

1 Roll out a thick layer of white clay after conditioning. Place a layer of liquid clay over the white clay and add iridescent Mylar flakes, known as "snowflake," over the surface of the clay.

2 Gently press the flakes down as flat as possible with a needle or knitting tool.

Bake the clay for the recommended time and temperature for the thickness you are working with.

3 Coat the surface with a layer of UV resin and cure under a UV lamp or in the sun, according to the manufacturer's directions. If you are coating clay that isn't contained within a bezel or with a clay border, coat the surface but take care to avoid overflow.

Remove any air bubbles before curing, as directed in the resin instructions. It may take several layers of resin, added and cured between applications, to completely cover the flake and get a smooth, glasslike finish. Keep in mind that the more layers you add, the more of a rounded cabochon effect you'll achieve. This can be quite pleasing visually. If a more level surface is desired, it's best to work with a setting or border around the faux opal clay.

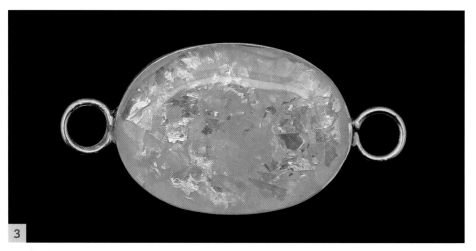

Faux Turquoise

This semiprecious stone is the ideal inspiration for creating beads, jewelry, and accessories using polymer clay. Colors of turquoise vary considerably from aqua and teal to sky blue and green, plus some colors in between. As different brands of clay offer varied color palettes, you may find it will take a bit of experimenting and even blending to achieve the shades of turquoise you desire. The method recommended here offers one of the most commonly seen shades of turquoise.

Also, the matrix found in turquoise can vary from fine to large cracks. The size to which you chop your clay will determine the finished result. In the end, well-executed faux turquoise will fool even the most discriminating of experts, plus it will be lighter in weight and much less expensive than its authentic counterpart.

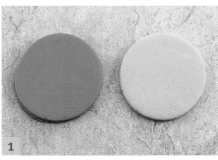

1 This recipe calls for a ratio mix of one part Peppermint clay to one part Sahara. Mix the clay thoroughly until blended.

2 Chop the clay into small pieces. Recompress the pieces into the size and shape you desire using your hands or a mold form. Do not blend the pieces back together when compacting. The clay should be pressed together to form a solid piece that is firm but still has cracks and crevices in the surface. Bake for the recommended time and temperature.

3 When the clay has cooled, rub burnt or raw umber paint into the cracks and crevices. Wearing disposable gloves is recommended for this step. Wipe away the excess paint with a dry paper towel and allow the rest of the embedded clay to dry completely. Follow with dry sanding using 600-, 800-, 1,000-, 1,500-, and 2,000-grit automotive-grade sandpaper and buff on a muslin wheel to a high shine.

tip

You can control the degree of crackling more easily by hand rolling and stretching.

TECHNIQUE #3

Faux Raku

Raku is a type of pottery that originated in Japan. Colors and finishes can vary greatly, but the most recognizable aspects of this type of earthenware are metallic accents and crackle finishes.

These can be achieved through the use of mica pigment powders for the metallic elements, and metal leaf and ink for the crackle finish.

1 For a crackle effect, use any color of metal leaf (not foil) applied to a sheet of white or cream-colored clay rolled through the largest setting of the pasta machine. Use an acrylic roller or progressively thinner settings of the pasta machine to get a crackle effect. For best results, do not stretch too much or create too much crackling. Finer lines are more realistic for this technique. Bake at the recommended temperature for 10 minutes.

2 Once the piece has cooled, dab black stamp ink (pigment or dye inks both work) over the entire surface area and rebake for 20 minutes. Once cool, lightly scrape the surface with the flat side of a clay blade or craft knife until the leaf is removed and the crackle effect is achieved.

tip

If you find that some of your crackle effect is scraped away, you can add some fine lines with a fine-tip permanent marking pen.

3 For metallic elements in your faux Raku, stipple two or more colors of metallic acrylic paint to the surface of black clay.

4 Allow the paint to dry and then press coarse sandpaper into the surface to texture. Bake the clay at the recommended temperature and time.

Both uncured and baked elements made using these techniques can be combined to create faux Raku projects like the piece seen at right.

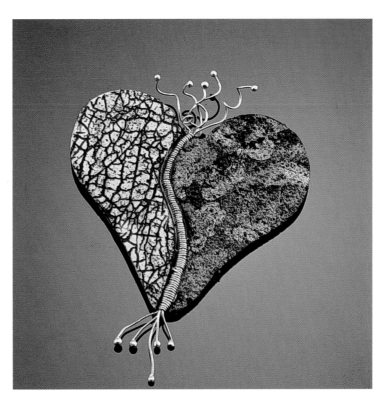

TECHNIQUE #4
Faux Ivory

Ivory has long been prized throughout the world for its use in making jewelry and decorative adornments. When one thinks of ivory, whale teeth and elephant tusks are usually what come to mind. Technically, any animal tooth or tusk is ivory, since these are composed of the same material as other bones. These days, legal ivory is typically the teeth, tusks, or bone from nonthreatened animal species. Otherwise, it's illegal to buy or sell ivory. It is still possible to legally purchase antique and fossilized ivories ranging from elephant tusks and whale teeth to fossilized mammoth, mastodon, and walrus tusks, but these ivories are very expensive.

Ivory also comes with varying degrees of visible layers and grades of quality and color. The "grain" or lined patterns typically found in ivory can range from non-

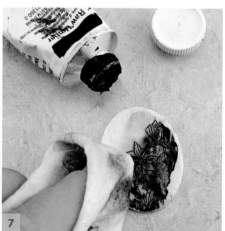

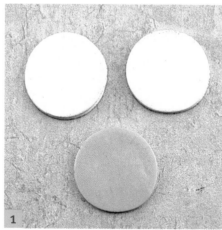

discernable to clearly layered in appearance. Lines can be uniform or random, depending on the specimen. Colors can range from nearly white to light yellow and brown tones.

Even deep cross sections of ivories that are tens of thousands of years old can be very fine in quality, not showing the antique quality that is expected with material this old (see the section of mammoth ivory in the far left photo on the facing page). The piece on the right was created on fossilized walrus tusk using traditional scrimshaw methods.

This recipe is created to make a rusticated ivory, one with more visible veining and a creamier tone. Play with different degrees of color and methods for these lines to find the formula that you like best.

1 Mix a ratio of two parts White to one part Ecru. Blend thoroughly.

2 Roll out translucent clay on the largest setting of the pasta machine without conditioning it. The edges should be a bit rough and crumbly. Tear or cut smaller pieces from the sheet of cream-colored clay made in the last step. Place these over that sheet with crevices showing between the pieces of translucent clay.

3 Roll the combined sheets through the pasta machine on the largest setting. Cut in half and stack. Repeat this step three more times.

4 Cut the sheet into quarters and stack. Compress with your hand or a roller.

5 Cut thin slices from this stack and lay side by side over a thin sheet of the cream-colored clay mixed in the first step. Roll together with an acrylic rod to meld the slices together and flatten. After rolling, this sheet can be thinned to a uniform thickness through the pasta machine.

6 Carve fine patterns into the clay with the tip of a needle before curing. Do not remove clay remnants before baking, as this can mar the surface. After baking, rub off any clay remnants from the carving process.

7 Rub raw umber acrylic paint over the clay and into the carving. Wipe off the excess paint with a dry paper towel.

8 Allow the rest of the paint to dry and follow with sanding and polishing as explained in | FINISHING, chapter 1, page 19 |. Another option is to stamp the surface of faux ivory sheets with inked stamps before or after baking.

Pictured below is a variety of faux ivory samples that best represents vintage and antiquated effects.

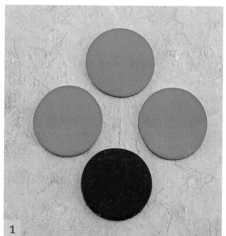

TECHNIQUE #5
Faux Cinnabar

Cinnabar (mercury sulfide) is a naturally occurring mineral that is found in both a reddish brick color and black. The red color is the most commonly known variety. This mineral was sometimes mixed to color the lacquer used in Asian lacquerware and other artwork. Due to its toxicity, cinnabar is now only made from dyed resin. It is generally carved or molded. It's easy to create close approximations of this lovely art form in clay.

1 Mix a ratio of three parts Indian Red with one part Chocolate until completely blended. (It's that simple!)

2 The clay can now be molded or stamped to make your cinnabar creations. Polishing by sanding and buffing will give a realistic finish.

TECHNIQUE #6
Faux Rust

The popularity of altered, distressed, and recycled artwork that began in the 1990s continues today. People's greater consciousness of our dwindling natural resources, combined with an appreciation of materials that survive the test of time, has increased our interest in found objects.

We used to fight the corrosion of metals, but now we have grown to love the natural patina of time—otherwise known as rust. This process is deliberately accelerated (or simulated) in the manufacture of furniture and home décor to create the illusion of artifacts. Fortunately, this look can easily, and more convincingly, some would say, be simulated with polymer clay.

The following directions stray slightly from what most package instructions will tell you. Here, the two-part finish is modified to achieve the look of "instant" rust on polymer clay. Also, this section just shows how to create a basic rusted finish. Other additives to the metallic base primer are available to create patinas found on other metals like copper and bronze. The base primer contains metal particles that will rust when the accelerator is added.

This technique is ideal for those who love to create assemblage, altered, and found-object art.

Hard to believe, but it's less expensive to make old keys and hardware and other items with polymer clay than it is to buy them. I've learned that as the demand for vintage hardware and findings increases, so does the price. The method described below also offers the option for custom objects and size variations that may not otherwise be available.

1 Black clay works the best for basic rusted objects. After thoroughly stirring the metallic base primer, apply a thick coat over the baked clay object of your choice. Air-dry this coat or place in the oven at 265°F until dry.

2 Restir the primer and add a second, thinner coat. After it begins to dry for a few minutes, apply a generous amount of the rust finish (accelerator) with a brush or cotton swab. This can be air-dried overnight or accelerated by baking at 265°F until dry.

3 If there is not enough rust after Step 2, apply another coat of the rust finish and air-dry or bake. Multiple applications of the rust finish can be added and dried until you achieve the desired finish.

4 Protect the finish of the rusted clay with a coat of matte sealer made for the rust product you are working with and allow to air-dry.

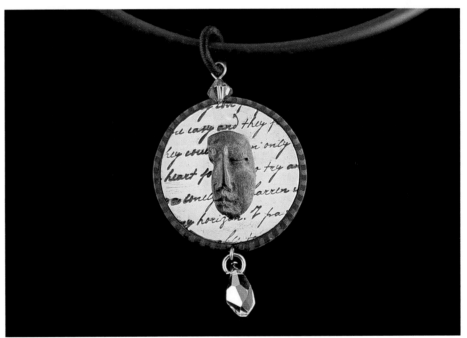

CHAPTER TEN

Stamping

USING A RUBBER STAMP WITH POLYMER CLAY is one of the most versatile ways to create visual interest on the surface of your work. Just as with many clay techniques, there are too many options to list in a single chapter, but this overview should have you well on your way to getting beautiful results while offering instant creative gratification.

If you've been reading other portions of this book before venturing into this chapter, you'll have realized that stamping (like other techniques and applications) appears in other sections and projects. As a crossover tool, stamping is unparalleled in its ability to offer so many different results.

The fact that polymer clay is a tactile medium is just one of its many attractions. Rubber stamps only add to this appeal by offering a controlled method for delivering exacting patterns and treatments. Is it any wonder that this medium, more than any other I have found, is responsible for bringing out the artistic passion of so many?

We've already explored the use of stamps for creating Mokumé Gané | see MOKUMÉ GANÉ, chapter 6, page 72 |, and this section will reexamine the use of stamps as a nondimensional surface treatment | see IMAGE TRANSFERS, chapter 5, page 62 |. This section will delve deeper into stamps as a means of adding texture and uniqueness to your work.

TECHNIQUES

- Basic Sutton Slice Sheet
- Advanced Sutton Slice Concepts
- Textile Effect
- Faux Tapestry

Even though many of the stamped examples and projects in this book feature stamps from my signature texture line, I encourage you to look to stamps you may already have available in your creative collection and be open to new designs.

Stamp Care

Taking care of your stamps is one of the most important components to creating beautiful results. Make sure the stamp is very clean before applying any pigment or powder. Stamps can be cleaned with products specifically designed for this purpose or with dish soap and a scrub brush. Some inks are indelible and may need a solvent-based cleaner to dissolve the ink. Grandma's Secret Rubber Stamp Cleaner® is a new product that is nontoxic and non-solvent-based. It does an excellent job of cleaning stamps.

It's not unusual that a stamp's rubber becomes stained over time, but the primary residue should be removed, and the sooner the better. It may take more than one application of cleaner to remove ink.

Wipe the stamp immediately with a paper towel or baby wipe and follow with cleaner. Apply a second application if needed, allowing a saturated application to sit for several minutes before wiping it away with a new towel.

Scrubbing a stamp with a drop of dishwashing detergent is a great way to remove all traces of mica pigments or other powders.

Store stamps away from direct sunlight when not in use. Since the rubber has a naturally tacky quality, it's advisable to store stamps in a drawer or container to prevent airborne dust and residue from accumulating.

Nondimensional Surface Stamping

This method delivers patterns to smooth, flat clay surfaces without the benefit of texture. Ink, paint sticks, and powders can all be applied to stamps and transferred onto both uncured and baked polymer clay.

When stamping baked clay, a heat curing of several minutes is recom-

Try stamping on gradient or other treated clay backgrounds in addition to using single-colored sheets.

You can even stamp over image transfers or clay treated with foil and leafing. Any type of rubber stamp can be used for surface stamping.

mended to permanently fix the ink or paint. The transfer of the stamp's pattern is usually easier to deliver to uncured rather than cured clay.

Photo-plate-style stamps that don't offer much in the way of dimension are ideal for this application, but don't forget that deeply patterned stamps can offer great results to clay surfaces. Play with stamping light backgrounds with sepia, pastel, or chalk inks before overstamping with bolder images and pigments for dramatic results.

General Stamping Guidelines

- After rolling the clay through a pasta machine, roll a few times with an acrylic rod to remove any ripples.

- Use fresh stamp pads to ensure even, allover coverage.

- Make sure you're working on a flat, smooth, hard surface when stamping.

- When working with unmounted stamps, it can sometimes be easier to apply the clay to the stamp as opposed to stamping the clay. Place the clay sheet on a piece of deli or parchment paper before smoothing it with a rod. This will help the clay adhere to the sheet, making it easier to handle. Place the clay down over the treated stamp.

- Lightly burnish the back of the clay with the flat side of your index finger to imprint the surface treatment onto the clay. Be careful not to use too much pressure, which can cause the clay to shift and the pattern to smear. If this occurs, flip the clay over and repeat until you get satisfactory results. Carefully lift the clay from two corners so that it can be raised in a single motion to prevent smudging.

- When possible, allow the ink (or paint) to dry before handling the clay. It can sometimes be difficult to tell when the ink is dry. In some cases, the drying time for the ink may be longer than the open (conditioned) time of the clay. This means that the ability to mold or form the clay without cracking can be compromised when positioning on non-flat surfaces.

- Placing clean deli paper over the stamped clay allows for immediate handling. You can carefully shape, or conform, the clay to a variety of surfaces if you use the paper as a protective barrier while the ink is still wet.

- Be careful that the paper doesn't shift, which can also smear the stamping. Some of the ink may transfer onto the paper, but this is usually not enough to mar the imprint. If you need to reposition the deli paper during this process, use a fresh piece.

- When applying pigmented mica powder to stamps, the surface must be as clean as possible and completely dry. Add powder to your fingertip. Tap off any excess powder into the container's lid before patting the surface of the stamp.

- Excess powder can fall into the crevices of the stamp, transferring it onto the clay in areas other than where the desired pattern should make contact. Try stippling (patting) different colored powders over the stamp.

- Apply a single color at a time to random spots, cleaning your finger between powders to prevent cross-color contamination in your containers. You might also play with applying different colored powders in stripes or graduated tones to the stamp.

- Add dimension to surface-stamped images and patterns by introducing texture to either the stamped or the negative areas on the clay's surface. Let the ink dry before texturing whenever possible. Stippling with a ball-tipped stylus or the end of a needle tool can create tremendous visual interest in your work.

The Sutton Slice

Earlier in this century, Pete Sutton, who worked in the creative arts industry, allowed me to turn him on to the wonders of polymer clay. We became fast friends. Pete couldn't get enough of the medium. Within a few weeks of "claying around," he was attempting a new concept for making mica-shifted clay.

Unfortunately, the idea, while good, didn't work for a number of reasons. Plus, it created a mess with a stamp he was using. In trying to clean the stamp,

he used scrap clay to grab the embedded clay from the face of the stamp. What he discovered was incredible!

Removing the embedded polymer created a contrasting dimensional pattern on the surface of the scrap clay. *Voila!* The Sutton Slice (the name for this technique, which was coined by my foster daughter and fellow polymer clay artist Anne Igou) was born!

This is the perfect example of how great discoveries are usually the result of a mistake. Be on the lookout for your own happy accidents!

One problem we had after he showed me the concept was getting consistent, reproducible results. I was so enamored of the idea, I devoted a couple of weeks to working with the concept in order to develop methods and tips that made it a viable technique. The technique itself is quite simple and straightforward, but it takes dedicated practice to get it down and perfect the results. I find this technique, much like the Mica Shift, to have a very meditative, Zen-like quality. It demands patience and a willingness to hone your blade skills.

TECHNIQUE #1

Basic Sutton Slice Sheet

1 Embed a small amount of conditioned clay into the stamp, pressing it firmly with your finger.

2 Hold the blade down firmly with your nondominant hand at one end. Bend the opposite end of the blade upward in an arch that presses the edge down firmly over the rubber. If the stamp is a high-grade quality, this won't shave off any of the rubber! Pull the blade through the raised clay that was just embedded, leaving it flush with the surface of the stamp **a**.

This is done with a pivoting motion. The end of the blade you are holding down should remain stationary, while the arched end of the blade moves in a circular motion as you slice **b**.

3 Continue adding small amounts of clay until the desired area has been filled and sliced. As you build the filled area, small amounts of clay may stick to your blade while slicing and be unintentionally removed.

Patch these areas until all the openings are filled. Check your blade frequently to make sure there is no clay stuck to it. Wipe the blade often to remove residue that can also drag the clay out of the stamp.

4 Once you are sure the desired area is completely filled, reshave the surface of the rubber with very firm pressure until all visible clay is removed from the raised surface of the rubber. Any clay residue will be transferred onto the substrate (base) layer of clay that becomes the background of the Sutton Slice sheet. During this final filling step, it's not unusual for some clay to come out. Repeat Steps 3 and 4 until the crevices are filled entirely and the surface is completely clean.

5 Roll out a conditioned sheet of clay large enough to cover the filled area. The thickness of the sheet depends on the application. Sheets thinner than the fourth-largest setting of the pasta machine are prone to tearing and may be too thin.

When just starting out, it's advisable to work with thicker settings (largest, second-largest, or third-largest) until you are comfortable with the technique.

6 Place the sheet down over the filled stamp. Spray a small amount of automotive protectant spray over the faceup side of the clay backing and spread it with your finger. This prevents your fingers from sticking to the clay and prematurely lifting it.

7 Tamp the clay down with your fingertips very firmly over the entire sheet. Continue this step until you have pressed the same areas of the entire sheet several times. Roll over the clay sheet one time only, using an acrylic rod with firm pressure. Do not roll back and forth! This can prematurely remove the clay from the stamp.

8 Wipe the automotive spray residue from the backing sheet with a paper towel.

9 Turn the stamp (with the clay still in place) down over a tile work surface. Press the stamp down firmly to adhere the clay to the tile.

10 In this step, the stamp is removed from the clay and not the other way around. **Do not pull the clay off the stamp!** Much of the clay will remain stuck inside. It's advisable to stand during this step in order to see the clay as you remove the stamp.

11 Bend the stamp backward, nearly folding it in half. Slowly roll it backward while you do this until you see the clay's edge. While holding the stamp (folded back) in place with one hand, use the other hand to press the edge of the clay down firmly against the tile. This area will be cut away when you trim, so don't worry about the distortion.

12 Slowly roll the stamp backward with one hand, pressing the stamp down just under the curled area as you continue. If you see an area where the clay remains in the stamp, you can slowly roll the stamp back in place and press the area with very firm pressure to fuse the clay background and embedded area together. Repeat this as needed until the clay comes out onto the background. See the tips section on page 119 for clay that won't budge from the stamp.

Continue until the entire pattern has been released. Lightly pat down the raised clay to ensure it is making contact with the background sheet. Trim and apply as desired toward the completion of your project.

Note the tonal contrast between the two samples in the photo below. Both were created using the same two colors (FIMO Soft Metallic Sapphire Blue and White). By embedding the lighter color and using darker background clay, as in the sample on the left, the effect is decidedly brighter than the sample on the right, where the colors were reversed.

Advanced Sutton Slice Concepts

Once you've mastered this method, try your hand at getting different effects.

A few ideas include using sheets of clay with a crackled foil or leafed background. You might try stamping a pattern on the background clay before pressing it onto the embedded sheet for a peek-through effect.

Keep in mind that the addition of other materials on the backing layer can act as a resist, making it difficult for the two clays to adhere to one another. This will also make it harder for the clay to release cleanly from the stamp. The effects are well worth the risk, but it's not for the faint of heart.

Another idea is to use a gradient background sheet of clay instead of a solid-colored one. A bit trickier, but fun to do, is to embed pieces of clay from a Skinner Blended sheet, as seen in the photo below in a case that was created with my "splat" stamp.

To achieve this effect, cut a gradient sheet rolled through the thickest setting of the pasta machine in a grid formation to create tiny tiles of clay. Begin with the lightest color and fill the stamp with rows of graduated color. Keep in mind that, as you move beyond the first colored row, the clay from the next darkest row may pick up some lighter clay when sliced.

Do not add this clay back into the stamp. Set it aside and start with a fresh clay "tile" from the grid to prevent color contamination from occurring as the additional rows of color darken. It's okay if you see color contamination occur on the back-filled clay that faces you. You won't see this when you release the clay from the stamp.

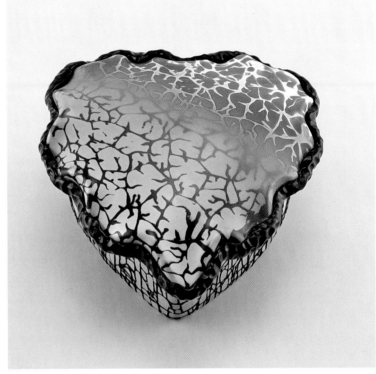

Some more advanced challenges include using more than one color in individual sections of the stamp. This effect can be seen on the notepad cover in the left photo above or the | SUTTON SLICE "About Face" Case project on page 182 |.

The ultimate Sutton Slice challenge is creating a raised gradient pattern against a gradient background. You can work with different colors and play dark ends against dark ends or oppose the light and dark ends as with the heart vessel shown in the right photo above. The Textile Effect (see page 121) was incorporated to turn the sheet used into a nondimensional surface.

Helpful Sutton Slice Tricks

• A clean, dry stamp is essential! This can't be stressed enough.

• Not all stamps will work with this technique. Stamps with a lot of depth work best. A lack of depth and/or too much detail can prevent the technique from working. Stamps with depth, but those that have extremely busy patterns, are harder to work with. Some small details may be lost, but this often isn't a problem as long as the larger areas of the pattern are properly filled and released.

• Stamps with a great deal of depth but extremely large patterned areas can be hard to shave after filling. As you practice, you'll find which types of patterns and depths work best for you. I designed most of my texture stamps with this and the Mica Shift techniques in mind.

• Mounted stamps can work for this technique, but the clay has to be pulled off, and it's common for areas to remain embedded. Ways around this are to remove the wood block mounting from your stamps and use an after-market acrylic mounting system. This will allow you the versatility of using your stamps both mounted and unmounted. This is what I've done with hundreds of my stamps. It takes much less room to store my stamps. Also, you may be surprised to find that you prefer to use your stamps unmounted for most applications, as I do!

- Ways of dealing with mounted stamps include baking the Sutton Slice clay in the stamp and removing when cool. However, this will prevent you from being able to bend or form the Sutton Slice sheet.

- Blades should be very clean and sharp. A flexible blade works best. Older blades with notches along the edge will make shaving the clay tricky.

- Use only small amounts of clay at a time. Embedding too much of the clay at one time can make proper shaving difficult, if not impossible.

- Softer clay works better than firmer brands. Also, when embedding larger areas, the open time for clay can be exhausted. This can result in the embedded clay being a bit dry and crumbly. This can be a desired effect | see TEXTILE EFFECT on the facing page |.

- Wipe fingers often with a baby wipe. Built-up residue can cause you to remove embedded clay when you are pressing a new area into the stamp. You may also spray a little bit of automotive protectant spray on the corner of your work tile. Periodically tap your finger into the spray to act as a resist agent while you are embedding the clay. Make sure you don't get this inside the stamp, as it can inhibit the clay from sticking. Remember, we want the clay to stick in the stamp, not on your fingers!

- When pieces of clay stick inside the stamp, no matter how well you fold the stamp, you can try to remove them with the tip of your craft knife or a needle tool and position them on the background sheet. I recommend baking the embedded clay in the stamp for 10 minutes to harden it before removing it and pressing it into the background clay. Add a tiny dot of liquid clay to the back of these pieces before pressing them in place. This will fuse the clays together more securely. This tip will also make it easier to remove and place the clay without damaging it.

- Every once in a while, you may miss a small area that didn't get filled after the baking has been done. Typically, this area is raised, just like the contrasting clay that was successfully embedded, only the color is that of the background sheet. Here, I think it's okay to cheat a little. I touch up these areas with permanent marker or matching acrylic paint. No one will know except you. I always say, "Fake it until you bake it!"

Textile Effect

This is a technique modified from the Sutton Slice. Once again, surprising discoveries often are the genesis of new techniques. In this case, I was rolling my Sutton Slice scraps through my pasta machine to blend and recondition. I noticed that repeated passes through the machine flattened the pattern until it looked like fabric, thus the name: Textile Effect. The result reminded me of the monochromatic look of textiles used to make some varieties of Hawaiian shirts.

1 When flattening a Sutton Slice sheet, it's important to use a background sheet of clay that's been rolled through the thickest setting of your machine.

2 When you have released the Sutton Slice, gently stretch it by hand before rolling it through the largest setting of the pasta machine. This is important, as it opens the background pattern and prevents the raised clay from folding over onto it during the gradual flattening stage. Stretch the clay gently in all directions during this step to avoid distorting the pattern.

3 While rolling, hold the end of the sheet with a little bit of tension to help the pattern stretch. Do not hold it too tightly, as this may cause the sheet to tear while rolling.

4 Repeat Steps 2 and 3, rolling the sheet through thinner and thinner settings until completely flat. Distortion can be adjusted by hand stretching after the final rolling.

When working with stiffer clays, the Textile Effect often shows crackling along the edges of the embedded clay after flattening. This is a way to achieve a faux batik effect.

Another option is to let the embedded clay sit inside the stamp overnight before removing it with a background sheet. This allows the clay to lose its open time, causing it to stiffen and crack when flattening. Keep in mind that when the clay is stiffer, it is also harder to get the background and embedded clays to adhere and thus release from the stamp.

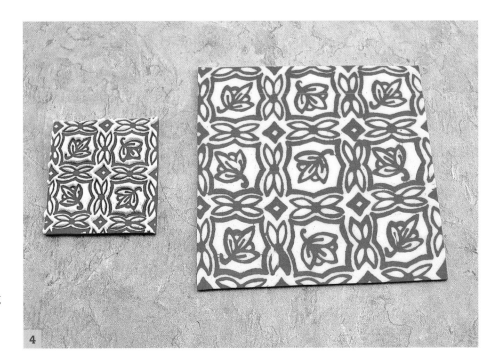

4

Faux Tapestry

Even though this is a faux technique, it's an offshoot of | THE SUTTON SLICE, page 114 | and the | TEXTILE EFFECT, page 121 |. Patting a contrasting mica pigment powder over the raised area of the stamp and then flattening it, as in steps 1–4 of the Textile Effect, achieves this look.

The outcome is a shadowed effect that appears to have the quality of interwoven threads. This is especially true when creating the technique with warm and metallic tones. I dubbed it Faux Tapestry, since my first experiments were done using a combination of warm and metallic tones, which reminded me of the look found in antique European tapestries.

A more dramatic crackle effect can be achieved with this technique by applying a layer of tempera or acrylic paint and stretching after the paint has dried.

Additional Embossed-Clay Effects

Here are a few more suggestions for getting different effects with embossed clay.

• After stamping the clay, pat mica pigment powder on the raised surface. This will leave the recessed areas in a contrasting relief. As with the application of powder to the rubber stamp mentioned earlier, you can create interesting results with striped, graduated, or stippled powder applications.

- Apply mica pigment powder to the raised surface of clay that was embellished with the Pavelka Peel technique | see LEAF AND FOILING EFFECTS, chapter 8, page 90 |. You might try using a color of powder that contrasts with the foil used or coordinate your tones by using matching powder shades, as used with the leaf border seen on the dish in the top right photo.

- Create an antique effect on stamped clay by rubbing acrylic paint into the crevices and over the entire surface. Follow by wiping it away. For a deeper tone, use a dry paper towel. Use a baby wipe to remove more paint while it's wet or to lighten the effect after drying.

The look of hand-tooled leather on the card case as shown in the bottom right photo was created by antiquing clay embossed with my "tooled leather" stamp with raw umber acrylic paint.

CHAPTER ELEVEN

Assembly, Formation, and Structure

THIS CHAPTER IS DEVOTED TO TECHNIQUES and treatments that involve assembly, formation, and structure of your work. Some of these concepts stand alone, such as mosaics and carving. Others may be elements or embellishments that make up only a portion of your work.

The use of the concepts can be deeply gratifying. They lend themselves to a wide range of applications from large-scale home décor to jewelry.

Mosaics

This is one of my favorite clay applications. Mosaics are works of art composed of tile. My first exposure to mosaics was to ancient artworks that date back to biblical times. Being fortunate to see these firsthand during my teen years began a longstanding love affair with this art form that continues to this day.

I have sought out mosaics during my travels and never cease to marvel at the complexity achieved by the earliest artists with the crudest of tools and resources. Mosaics share a close similarity with one of my favorite painterly concepts, pointillism, which is a two-dimensional way of creating images with small dots of color (charcoal, pastel, or paint).

The beauty of making polymer clay mosaics over more traditional methods (including ceramic tile, glass, and more recently china or pottery shards) is that you have total control over every aspect of your creation.

TECHNIQUES

- Three-Step Mosaics
- Carving
- Hollow Forms
- Pillow Forms
- Puff Forms
- Nontwist Suspension Method for Hanging Puff Forms
- Flowers
- Ribbon Roses
- Layered Roses
- Cutter Boxes
- Stencil Frames

In creating your tiles, you can determine the size, color, shape, and thickness of each piece. You can even control whether or not the tiles are flat or dimensional.

In most cases, you may prefer to use my three-step, no-mess method for creating polymer clay mosaics. The exception would be the creation of large-scale projects that cannot be cured in an oven, such as the fireplace surround I created in our family room in 1999 (below).

This section addresses basic mosaic creation. You can go beyond the basics, though, and try to spread your artistic wings by working with gradient-blended, stamped, molded, and cutter-shaped tiles.

Three-Step Mosaics

This technique is so named because the formation of the design and grouting occur in three simple steps. Before creating the actual mosaic, you must first make your tiles. Determine the details needed, including overall size and colors.

Keep in mind that while the basis of traditional pictorial mosaics involves square tiles, corners and curves are often filled in with triangles and trapezoids. You may also need to cut tiles down to smaller squares to complete the pattern. These additional shapes and sizes are easily cut from the basic clay tiles after curing.

Traditional mosaics are laid out in a freehand or mechanically drawn design over a foundation. They are attached with mastic (adhesive). After setting up, grout is pressed into the crevices and wiped away from the surface. This can be a messy job. The three-step technique makes the process cleaner and quicker.

The use of polymer clay tiles for large, nonbakeable surfaces (such as my fireplace) must be done in the traditional manner. I would not recommend polymer clay for outdoor mosaics. The lifespan of the clay can be affected adversely by harsh weather conditions. Clay is best suited to projects that remain indoors.

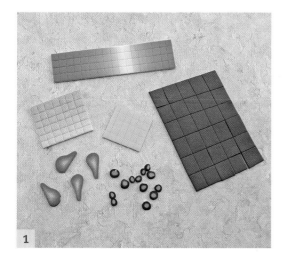

This tabletop measures 1 sq. ft. and includes nearly 2,000 handmade polymer tiles.

1 Start by creating your tiles. Since the grout is a base layer of polymer clay that's been rolled through the largest setting, the recommended thickness for tiles is the third- or fourth-thickest setting. Thicker tiles will be hard to embed deeply enough and will be difficult to cut down. Thinner tiles can be prone to popping out and may break when pressed into the base, or grout.

Roll out solid-color or gradient sheets to the desired thickness. Score with a clay blade in a grid pattern at the size you prefer. Since most of my mosaic work tends to be 12 in. by 12 in. or smaller, I create tiles that range in size from about ¼ in. square to micro tiles that measure only 2 mm to 3 mm square.

Bake the scored sheet for at least 20 minutes. When the clay cools, you can snap the tiles apart by hand. Making triangles and other shapes can be easily done with a craft knife.

2 Draw or trace your design onto tracing or deli paper. Place the paper over a layer of clay (grout) that has been rolled through the thickest setting of the pasta machine. Cut through the lines with the tip of the craft knife **a**.

When you remove the paper, your design will be incised into the grout layer. This layer can be any color you desire, but black offers the greatest contrast. The grout clay can also be attached to any bakeable surface you are covering beforehand, as shown with the covered pillbox here **b**.

3 Press your tiles into the design, starting from the center and working your way out.

Keep in mind, as you press tiles into place, that some of the grout layer will

expand outward, causing the very edge of your design to be slightly smaller than the drawing. Normally, a row or two of tiles may be lost as a result.

When all the tiles are in place, place anything with a hard, flat surface over the top of the mosaic and press down with firm, even pressure to seat the tiles more securely. Trim the edges of whatever you have covered and bake for 30 minutes.

This mosaic mirror frame is an example of using specifically shaped clay cutters to make foil-covered tiles. The effect can either be a more exacting geometric pattern or freeform.

This trinket box, featuring micro tiles, was based on an embossed pattern made in the clay grout using a rubber stamp. These are only a few options to consider when creating mosaics with polymer clay.

TECHNIQUE #2

Carving

Carving is a fun way to create dimensional surface patterns in layered polymer clay. Carving is done with fine V-shaped Speedball® cutters. This is the same tool that many secondary school art classes use in the creation of linoleum and wood block carvings.

There are two basic methods for creating carved clay. Both involve the use of one or more very thin (thinnest setting of the pasta machine) layers of clay over one thicker layer.

Choose colors of clay with significant contrast. Adding a thin layer of white between the top and bottom layers will help the design pop more visibly.

1 Select the uppermost color to carve through and roll out the clay on the thinnest setting. Smooth this over a sheet of the base layer (to be revealed) using your finger. Apply the clay at one end and work your way down to the other to make sure that all air is pressed out as you layer the sheets.

If a middle layer of white is desired, start with this sheet first (rolled through the thinnest setting) and follow by adding the top sheet. Roll the layered sheets through the largest setting of the pasta machine.

2 You now have two options for carving. The first option is to carve your clay before baking. It's helpful to use a design drawn onto tracing or parchment paper, as with the mosaic technique, and lightly cut through it to incise your design first.

The other option is to bake the clay and carve afterward. Carving before baking is easier. Only carve the basic outlines of the design, those that you want the underlying color to show through.

3 Surface carvings are more easily made by impressing a needle tool or a ball-tip stylus into the design first.

Want a more challenging project? Braver souls can try freehanded carving with this technique.

tip

Using a larger blade or recarving through exposed lines after baking can expand the width or deepen lines, if desired. Reveal beautiful gradient or patterned carvings by using Skinner Blended or patterned sheets of clay for your underlying layers.

Hollow Forms

Constructing hollow forms allows the artist to create a variety of dimensional shapes that are lighter and more challenging than solid forms. While there are other means of achieving hollow forms, this section is an introduction to using cutters to create two kinds of forms.

The first types of forms have one domed and one flat side. I call these puff forms. We'll refer to the second variety, which have a domed shape on two opposing sides, as pillow forms. When pillow forms are made using circles, they are often referred to as "lentils."

These constructions can be used primarily as pendants, charms, or surface embellishments. They can be made in just about any shape you can find cutters for. The amount of doming can be subtle or extreme, depending on the desired outcome.

The clay sheets used can simply be in a solid color, or they can be marbled, stamped, Skinner Blended, embossed, or Sutton Sliced.

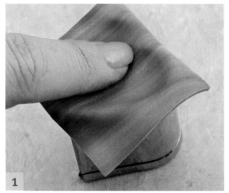

Sheets of clay need to be slightly larger than the outer edges of whichever cutter you are working with. The clay thickness is best set on the third- or fourth-thickest setting. Thicker sheets will be difficult to work with when forming the dome shape, and thinner sheets can tear too easily.

1 Place the cutter upside down on your work/baking tile. Lay the sheet down over the sharp edge of the cutter. Gently press the clay down to seal it onto the edges without cutting through the clay. Carefully press the clay down in the center to form the dome.

Continue smoothing the clay down along the outer edges of the cutter to expand the dome shape until you get the desired concave depth. Do not overstretch the clay, which may cause it to tear. If you notice the sides on the cutter edge beginning to tear, stop deepening the clay or use a lighter touch.

2 Bake the clay in place on the cutter for 20 minutes. Use a heat-protective mitt or pad for this step. When the cutter is very warm to the touch (not hot!), turn it right side up with the clay still in place. With the clay sitting on the tile, press the cutter down over the clay **a**. Use the oven mitt to apply very firm pressure so that the cutter goes through the clay. Depending on the thickness of the clay, this step may not cut all the way through. If that happens, just remove the cutter and cut through the score marks with a craft knife **b**.

3 One other option for creating round, hollow shapes is to place circular-cut clay sheets over the top of regular incandescent (not halogen) light bulbs and bake. This creates a nice, subtle curvature in the clay for lower-profile pillows and puffs.

TECHNIQUE #4
Pillow Forms

Two identically shaped clay domes are attached together to create hollow forms with dimension on both sides. To achieve matching edges, sand the bottom of each dome on 600-grit paper over a flat, firm surface until the edges meet perfectly. These halves can now be connected with bonder glue. A little touch-up sanding along the edges will give the sides a nice rounded finish.

Sanding and matching edges can be very labor intensive. Another option for finishing the edges is to glue on a decorative border all the way around to conceal the seams (see bottom left photo). Possible treatments include textured or striped clay strips, overlapping cane slices, and foiled, molded, or rolled snake borders. This form was covered with a black clay strip and textured.

TECHNIQUE #5
Puff Forms

Glue domed clay shapes over a flat sheet of polymer clay that is slightly larger than the form. Trim the excess clay from the edges with the craft knife and rebake.

For jewelry applications, the puff can be mounted on another surface, or you can drill through the top or bottom or from side to side and thread wire or cording through to hang.

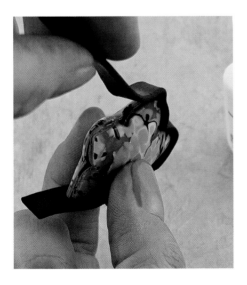

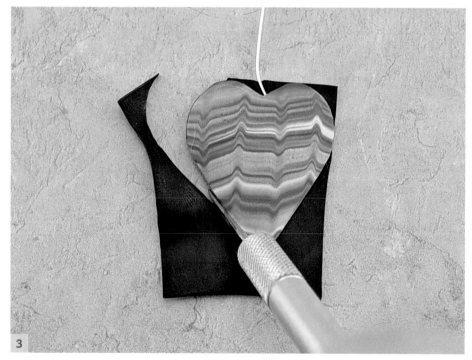

Nontwist Suspension Method for Hanging Puff Forms

1 Use round-nose pliers to bend one end of a wire, headpin, or eyepin back and forth, making U- or S-shaped curves (20-gauge to 24-gauge dead-soft wire is recommended). All the bends should be parallel to one another so that the piece lies flat after shaping. Press the wire into the bottom foundation of clay so that it is embedded flush with the surface of the clay.

2 Glue a ball of scrap clay down over the wire at any point that will be concealed by the puff top. Attach the puff to the base layer of clay with bonder glue.

3 Trim the excess clay and bake. After baking, either sand the edges to finish or cover with a decorative border and rebake.

TECHNIQUE #7
Flowers

Forming flowers by hand is a wonderful skill to have when the need for accents and embellishments is called for. You can create your flowers in any size, but I suggest you begin practicing larger constructions and get comfortable with the concept before attempting very small flowers. It's great that you can practice over and over with the same piece of clay.

If you like this concept, consult the Internet and gardening books for inspiration in creating dimensional flowers, but don't be afraid to create imaginary flower constructions as well.

As the formations tend to be delicate, stronger and more resilient clays are recommended for the creation of flowers | see POLYMER CLAY ESSENTIALS, chapter 1, page 6 |.

TECHNIQUE #8
Ribbon Roses

This is a very simple construction. For this technique, shorter lengths of clay are used to create rosebuds, whereas longer snakes of clay are used to create roses in full bloom. Making this flower is as easy as 1-2-3.

1 Flatten a snake of clay between your fingers. Further flatten one edge by pinching it very thin between your fingers. This side will be the outer edges of the flower's petals.

2 Roll the end of the snake in a spiral. Keep winding the spiral to the desired number of rotations, pinching off any excess length with your fingers.

3 Adjust the rose by pinching and bending the edges to give your flower a more realistic look **a**.

To finish off flowers for flat, surface applications, roll the base of the flower's stem between your fingers into a cone shape. Carefully slice underneath the flower with a clay blade to form a flat base. These can be attached to uncured or baked clay with bonder glue **b**.

Roses can also be attached with bonder glue to floral wire. Add clay leaves for a more realistic effect and bake at the recommended time and temperature.

It's handy to have several prebaked roses on hand for project embellishment.

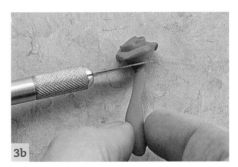

Layered Roses

These formations offer a more realistic look than ribbon roses, yet they are still surprisingly simple to create.

1 Start by forming a small ribbon rose-bud for the center.

2 Flatten three to seven balls of clay into discs between your fingers. As with ribbon roses, you'll want to pinch one side very thin to create the petal's edge.

3 Wrap the first petal around the rose-bud center. Pinch the outer edge together slightly in the center at the top and gently roll the edge downward. Study photos of roses to see how the petals take this shape when in full bloom.

4 Continue to add as many petals as you like, depending on the size and blossoming stage you are looking to achieve. Pressing the petals inward toward the center will give the look of a rose that isn't in full bloom. Wrap these at staggered intervals around the outside of the flower formation. Adjust each petal before adding the next.

Now that you have some experience with making roses, move on to making them with Skinner Blended bull's-eye cane slices for a more complex effect. Another idea includes using a brush to dust the outer edges of the petals with mica pigment powder.

Try your hand at other types of flowers. Clay cutters of different sizes and shapes can be helpful in the formation of other types of flower petals.

tip

The thinner the petals appear, the more realistic the results will be. This effect can be visible along the upper pinched edges, while the lower portion of the petals can remain thicker for added strength.

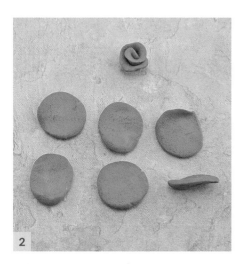

• Clay wrapped directly around metal is easier to remove if done while the clay and cutter are warm (not hot). Use light pressure all the way around when pushing the clay off the cutter. Ease the clay off slowly and gently.

• If the top edge isn't straight all the way around after baking, dry-sand the edges on 600-grit paper until it is level on all sides.

TECHNIQUE #10

Cutter Boxes

Metal cookie and canapé cutters make great forms for creating small structures or vessels. The concept is simple: Wrap clay around the outside of the cutter to create the body of the box.

To begin, select the cutter of your choice. When first making these types of formations, choose simpler shapes (circles, ovals, squares, and rectangles are a good way to start).

The conditioned sheets of clay should be fairly thick. The largest, second-largest, or third-largest settings of a pasta machine are recommended. Thinner settings can be too delicate, and the clay is prone to breakage when it's removed from the cutter.

Determine the desired height of the side walls for your vessel when cutting your clay sheet. This may be limited, based on the height of the cutter itself. Canapé cutters, which tend to be much taller than cookie cutters, are often a better choice for taller boxes.

When working with simpler shapes, it's possible to bake the clay directly on the cutter and remove after baking. However, wrapping a sheet of deli or parchment paper around the cutter first will create a nonstick barrier that makes removing the clay easier after curing.

1 Prepare a strip of clay that is longer than the circumference of your cutter. Make sure that the bottom edge is cut straight. Wrap the clay around the cutter with the straight edge lined up against the bottom of the cutter.

2 When the ends of the strip overlap, cut through the two layers with your blade at a 45-degree angle. Remove the excess ends of clay and smooth the angled edges together and blend until seamless.

2

3 Trim the upper edge of the strip with the clay blade to adjust the height of the side walls and to ensure that the upper edge is straight. Bake the clay on the cutter for 30 minutes at the recommended temperature. When cool, remove it from the cutter.

4 Glue the cooled box frame down over a layer of clay rolled out on the largest setting of the pasta machine. Press the frame down gently to slightly embed the edges. Trim the excess clay and bake the box for 15 minutes.

5 Use the cutter to cut out a piece of clay rolled through the largest setting of the pasta machine. Trim about 1/16 in. of clay from the edges of the piece to make it slightly smaller. This will be the inner portion of the lid that holds the upper-most portion in place.

6 Cut out a second piece with the cutter for the upper portion of the lid. Glue the inner clay shape to the center of the clay lid. Add a border treatment of your choosing along the edge. Bake for 25 minutes.

tip
Add a clay or decorative handle made from crystals or beads. The latter is easily attached with a head pin through a hole that can be made in the clay before or after baking.

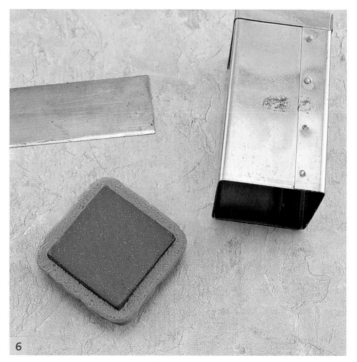

tip
Glue a decorative snake or molded border around the base to conceal the seam and enhance the finished appearance of your vessel.

Stencil Frames

This technique is a fun way to create elaborate, decorative frames that are lovely to use just as they are for ornaments or other adornments, or they can be backfilled with clay to get effects reminiscent of stained glass and enamel work.

Look for stencils with openings large enough to use a craft knife with. The pattern shouldn't be too busy or tiny. It's also helpful if the stencil doesn't have extremely thin lines between sections.

1 Roll out a sheet of the desired clay color slightly larger than the size of the stencil. The thickness should be the largest, second-largest, or third-largest setting of the pasta machine. Roll the clay down onto a clean, smooth tile so that it adheres well. Make sure there are no visible air pockets.

2 Press the stencil down over the clay firmly. Cut out the openings and remove the excess clay. You can fine-tune the edges by trimming the sides of the clay after baking.

3 Bake the clay with the stencil in place for 30 minutes. When the clay and stencil are cool, carefully slide the blade in between the two to separate them. Refine the surface by sanding to a matte or polished finish using wet-dry sandpaper. For polishing instructions | see POLYMER CLAY ESSENTIALS, chapter 1, page 19 |.

4 To backfill the frame, press conditioned clay into the opening and carefully slice off the excess with a clay blade. Use care when adding more than one color so you don't overlap these when filling the openings, as this can contaminate the other colors.

tip

Use one color at a time when filling and bake the frame for 10 minutes. After cooling, add the second color and bake, repeating until all the areas are filled with the colors of your choice. This helps prevent contaminating the other clay colors.

Scraping the baked clay with the flat edge of a craft knife will easily remove any color that accidentally gets on the wrong areas.

CHAPTER TWELVE

Surface Treatments

THIS CHAPTER FOCUSES ON manipulations and superficial treatments for altering the appearance of polymer clay. Basically, all techniques for polymer clay can be considered surface treatments since the goal is to create a finished piece. Other methods also address manipulations that can influence unseen aspects of a project's structure, but ultimately these, too, affect the visible aspects of your creations.

These are in addition to some treatments covered previously in greater depth, such as "Leaf and Foiling Effects" in chapter 8. You'll find techniques that are solely clay-based and others that take a mixed-media approach.

Many of these techniques lend themselves to accessorizing clay creations, but they can also stand alone as the focal element of your work. Enjoy mixing and matching these concepts with others found in this book.

TECHNIQUES

- Marbling
- Barber Pole Striping
- Border Treatments
- Stencil Gané
- Silk Screening
- Granulars

TECHNIQUE #1
Marbling

This technique offers an elegant finish to clay projects. It brings to mind decorative treatments for paper and fabric that date back centuries. Traditional marbling is a method of aqueous surface design whereby paint is floated on a solution, referred to as "size" or "on water." Paper or fabric is dipped below the surface, the paint is pulled and swirled, and then the paper or fabric is lifted to pick up the design.

While the process is different for polymer clay, marbling clay is incredibly simple, and the results are always beautifully mixed. Plus, marbling is a wonderful way to use scrap clay.

Follow these guidelines to create marbled sheets of clay.

- Twisting or folding snakes, chopped pieces, or scrap pieces of clay will create marbling. Twisting and folding can both be used (see the middle photo at

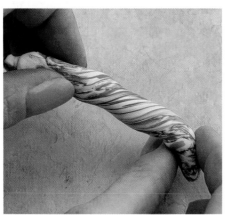

left), but don't overblend the clay or you will end up with very little marbling and possibly a solid color.

- Another option is to take a thick slice from compressed clay scraps, roll the slice into a snake, and twist before flattening through the pasta machine (see the bottom left photo at left).

- Feathering is a popular look in marbled treatments. Dragging lines into the clay's surface and then smoothing it flat achieves this look. Use a tool with a blunt point at the end, like a medium- to large-gauge knitting needle. Sharp points such as needle tools are too fine to effectively grab and smudge the clay.

- When dragging the lines in the surface, hold the tool almost parallel to the surface of the marbled clay. Slowly pull the tool across the surface in straight or wavy lines to create your pattern. The goal is to pick up clay as you draw the tool across the surface and drag it to form lines.

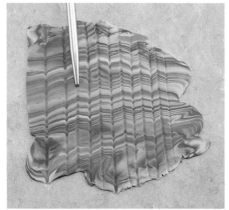

- To achieve the chevron feathered pattern seen in the puff bead heart pendant in the top left photo, drag straight vertical lines across the marbled clay sheet. Space the lines evenly apart. Turn the clay sheet 180 degrees and drag vertical lines between the first rows made in the opposite direction (see the bottom right photo at left). Flatten and smooth the clay sheet (adding a thicker backing sheet of white clay if needed).

Barber Pole Striping

Creating striped borders and edging adds a touch of elegance to any project. This can also be referred to as candy cane striping.

A fairly small striped snake will create a surprisingly large amount of length, depending on the diameter used. The example shown here has a bit of added flair by using some strips made from foiled clay.

1 Use the lightest color in your chosen palette to make the base snake. Roll thin sheets of the other clay colors (fifth- or sixth-largest setting of the pasta machine). Cut strips from these sheets and lay them lengthwise across the snake at varying intervals. Make sure to leave sufficient room between the strips to allow the base color to show through.

2 The technique is easy since it's not necessary to be perfect in creating the surface lines. Play with pattern variations. Placing strips of identical thickness at even intervals around the snake base will produce a different look than placing them with variable spacing will.

Using strips of varying thickness placed randomly around the snake base will also result in a completely different look.

3 Roll the snake to the desired length and diameter. The lines will appear distorted during this step. Don't worry; the distortion will disappear when twisting the clay. In this example, foiled clay strips are used for one of the colors.

4 Uniform spacing between the twists is achieved by holding the clay at one end while slowly twisting the other end a small amount at a time. Work your way down the snake gradually as you twist.

Do not hold the clay at both ends while twisting, as this will result in tight twists at the ends and wider rotations in the center.

The striping can be further adjusted by spot-twisting where needed. Reversing the twist can widen the spaced intervals of your stripes.

If necessary, lightly roll the snake after twisting to smooth out any ridges that form during this step.

rolling tips

- Dedicated practice is needed to be able to roll snakes of uniform thickness. It's well worth the effort to develop your rolling abilities with clay. I have spent hours of practice doing this and now seldom use an extruder. Some techniques, such as striped snakes, cannot be achieved with a barrel extruder.

- Most of us have problems rolling snakes because we use too much pressure with our fingers. Another problem is that we tend to roll with the heaviest pressure in our index finger. The pressure that is typically applied lessens as you move down to the middle, ring, and pinkie fingers. This results in raised ridges and lumps when the clay is rolled between fingers. A very light, even touch is all that is needed, along with the momentum created while rolling, to extend and reduce the clay.

- When your snake is the desired length and diameter, use your index finger to gently roll the thicker areas to a uniform diameter with the narrower areas of the snake.

- Rolling with a clear acrylic sheet or block can make snakes of uniform thicknesses. The snake can be rolled to the length of the acrylic piece you are working with but not longer, as the edge of the acrylic will emboss ridges into the clay. For the best results, hold the acrylic at both ends, which helps keep it more level. Using one hand to hold the block tends to roll the snake into a tapered shape. The diameter of the snake can be controlled by stacking even numbers of playing cards at each end of the block. The snake can only be reduced as thick as the cards are stacked in height.

Border Treatments

Oftentimes, a project calls for simple edging or a narrow border to give it a finished look. Smooth matte and polished borders are lovely but can be difficult to achieve due to handling the project when attaching clay. Of course, sanding and polishing are options for finishing baked clay, but this is sometimes too labor intensive.

To get a finished quality for edging without investing the time and trouble of sanding and polishing, consider solid clay colors or foiled edging that is textured. Several areas within this book look at using coarse sandpaper as one means of quick finishing, which also hides fingerprints, surface imperfections, and seams.

Another favorite treatment used in much of my work is "creping." The appearance is similar to that of crepe paper. This is achieved by pouncing or pressing a needle tool against the clay edge back and forth in the same spot several times. This is continued until the entire edge is "creped." The beauty of this method is that it's not important to get perfectly spaced impressions. The organic quality of the texture can be the perfect finishing touch for many surfaces and border treatments you create.

Stencil Gané

This is a discovery I made while playing with small metal stencils designed for paper embossing. I wanted small tiles with letters on them and found that this could be created in a manner similar to Mokumé Gané | see MOKUMÉ GANÉ, chapter 6, page 72 |. It can be done with patterned stencils as well. The resulting effect is crisp, clean impressions with a slightly raised surface.

1 Start by rolling a sheet of the top clay color through the thinnest setting of the pasta machine. Smooth this over a base layer of contrasting colored clay that's been rolled through the largest setting of the pasta machine. Cut the clay so it is slightly larger than the area of the stencil being used.

2 Spray a very generous amount of auto-motive protectant spray on the top clay layer and spread with your finger.

3 Press the clay onto the back of the stencil. Use enough force to push the clay out the front of the stencil. Carefully slice the extruded clay off the surface using a clay blade. If the only color showing isn't the base layer, push the clay through a bit more and slice again.

4 Gently peel the clay off the back of the stencil, and you'll have your design. Trim and use as desired.

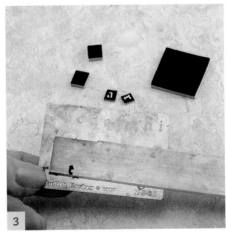

Silk Screening

This is a method of printing that forces ink or paint through a blocked mesh design onto fabric or paper.

Typically, a rubber squeegee or a roller is used to deliver a design through the open areas of a mesh design. The negative areas are coated with an impenetrable substance like a gel emulsion. Silk screening dates back about 1,000 years to the Song Dynasty of China, and it made its first appearance in Europe in the 16th century when silk became more readily available through trade.

Polymer clay pioneer Gwen Gibson is recognized for having popularized this technique for use on polymer clay. This method can be done using prepared screens available through Polymer Clay Express or customizable PhotoEZ screen print kits | see RESOURCE GUIDE, page 216 |. Custom or copyright-free black graphics and illustrations can be transferred onto PhotoEZ emulsion sheets and developed with sunlight and tap water.

With proper care (refer to package instructions), silk screens can offer many years of usability.

1 Prepare cleaning supplies before you begin (a pan of clean, warm water with a drop of mild detergent). Place the silk screen—emulsion (shiny) side down—over smooth, flat clay. Gently burnish the screen onto the clay to seal the edges of the open-weave design.

2 Apply a generous line of acrylic paint along one end of the screen. Quickly and firmly pull the paint across with a squeegee or a plastic card. Continue to move the paint over the design until you see that it has been spread in through the mesh openings. This step must be done in a matter of seconds, as the paint dries very quickly.

3 Pull the screen off the clay and place immediately in the pan of water. Gently use your fingers to rub the paint off the screen. Dried paint will ruin the silk screen, so the sooner the screen is cleaned, the better! Lay the clean screen between a few sheets of paper towels and blot to remove the excess water. Dry flat. The screen should only be reused when completely dry.

4 Allow the paint to dry before cutting, manipulating, or baking the clay. Depending on the use of your finished piece, sealing the clay with liquid polymer, resin, acrylic, or water-based Varathane is recommended to protect the design | see FINISHES, chapter 2, page 35 |.

Silk Screen Design Ideas

- Use multiple screens to apply a layered look with contrasting paint colors for backgrounds and foregrounds. The paint from a previous screen must be completely dry before adding secondary layered designs (see the photo at right).

- Texture the clay areas around the painted design with a stylus or other tool before baking to add dimensional variety to your work.

- The design can be left as a raised surface or rolled flat into the clay after drying for a nondimensional effect.

- Play with both metallic and solid colors for visual appeal in your creations.

TECHNIQUE #6

Granulars

Also known as inclusions, these can be any type of particle that can safely be baked when blended into or impressed onto the surface of polymer clay prior to baking. Some of the more popular inclusions include glitter and thermographic embossing powders. These can give clay varied finished effects from iridescent and metallic to stonelike or speckled | see the photos for CUTTER BOXES, chapter 11, page 135 |.

Granulars work extremely well in tinted and nontinted translucent clay, but don't be afraid to experiment with opaque clay colors. Typically, larger amounts of material need to be added to solid-color clays than to translucent varieties in order to be visible after baking.

When working with glitter, keep in mind that some types may not bake well. Large-flake economy glitter may actually dull or lose color during baking. Determine the finished effect by test-baking a small amount in your clay before you begin a project. Art Glitter works very well in polymer clay and comes in an amazing array of colors and effects | see RESOURCE GUIDE, page 216 |.

EMBOSSING POWDERS

Embossing powders (the type used with rubber stamp crafting) melt when baked in polymer clay. When well blended into clay, the effect is one of fine speckling on the surface. Some powders will have a matte finish, while others will be glossy.

Embossing powders may be solid colors or coated. Solid colors will retain the color after melting, but the coated type may be an entirely different color after baking than the color you mixed into the clay. Typically, the color of coated powders will end up being white or a lightly tinted shade of the original color after baking.

Test-bake embossing powder in a small amount of clay to see what the finished result will be before blending into larger amounts of clay. The left photo on the facing page shows the look of light blue embossing powder mixed into a disc of blue clay. The bottom disc in the same photo shows the effects after baking. Notice the powder has

"bloomed" to white, indicating that this is a coated powder.

Hand-mixing is always recommended when adding granular materials into your clay. You run the risk of contaminating or damaging your pasta machine when using it to blend inclusions into clay. Start with a small amount of the material and add more gradually, if needed, to achieve the material saturation desired.

Other inclusions to consider are organic and found materials including, but not limited to, spices, coffee, ground incense, dried herbs, pepper flakes, sand, and candy decorations. Adding many of these types of materials is a great way to create faux stone effects.

Keep in mind that large particles or large amounts of granulars can affect the baked surface, resulting in texture, regardless of how well they are mixed into the clay. This can be a desirable look, but a second baking with a layer of liquid clay or the addition of a resin coat can flatten the surface when required.

As with the recommendation for making color "chip charts," | see POLYMER CLAY ESSENTIALS, chapter 1, page 18 | you can make these discs with inclusions for future reference. Use a needle tool to etch the name of the material mixed into the clay and the type of clay on the back of the chip before baking.

FIBERS

Fibers are another type of inclusion that can be mixed or added to clay surfaces. These can be fine yarns or threads in long or cut strands. A beautiful material to use with polymer clay is Angelina Fiber. This is an incredibly fine material that is highly light reflective. Varieties of this material include metallic, holographic, and iridescent effects (see the top right photo above).

Small amounts of the material can be blended into clay by kneading. Another option is to spread a pinch of this featherweight material between two nonstick ironing sheets and iron on the cotton setting for a few seconds to flatten.

Do not overheat, as the material can burn very quickly, causing it to lose its light-reflective qualities. Sealing with liquid clay, resin, or a clay-safe varnish should protect Angelina Fiber on the surface of clay. A layer of Angelina Fiber can be seen underneath this clay-framed image transfer that is set under a coating of UV resin (see the photo directly above).

CHAPTER THIRTEEN

Finishing Touches and Final Thoughts

BASED ON THE MATERIAL INCLUDED in this book, along with all the potential variations and manipulations of common clay knowledge, I could have expanded on polymer clay concepts indefinitely! If only I had a few thousand more pages . . . .

The evolution of the polymer clay medium is still in its early stages. The future for this amazing material is bound to hold many more surprises. I have been privileged to play in clay long enough to see it run the gamut from a children's toy and hobby material to a recognized fine-art medium in world-renowned museums. It's exciting to see polymer clay come into its own.

I always say, "It's not the medium, but what you do with it that makes it art." In the end, how the medium is regarded is not as important as what it brings to your life. It is my hope that you have found this book helpful and inspiring.

By now you have realized that no single clay technique or concept need stand alone. The fun is in combining ideas and techniques to explore your own creative voice.

This chapter is devoted to a few ideas and techniques that will help round out your projects. After all, it's all in the details!

TECHNIQUES

- Scrap Clay
- Additional Thoughts on Molding
- Leafing Pens
- Suspending Clay
- Tube Attachments
- Fold-Over Bails
- Connecting Pieces to Jump Rings
- Fancy or Coil-Wrapped Loops

2

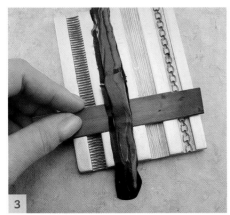

3

4a

Scrap Clay

When polymer clay remnants can be blended into a desirable color, this is not considered scrap clay. *Scrap* refers to mixed bits of clay (sometimes with inclusions, foil, leaf, or paint) that, when blended, become a muddy or gray color.

Those who have the clay bug in a serious way tend to accumulate pounds and pounds of scrap clay. Various sections of this book, have touched on techniques (junk cane and marbling) for utilizing scrap clay decoratively | see MILLEFIORI CANING, chapter 4, page 44 and SURFACE TREATMENTS, chapter 12, page 138 |.

Compressed blocks of scrap clay also lend themselves to the techniques found in | MOKUMÉ GANÉ, chapter 6, page 72. |

Also consider that scrap clay is great for using for the base of beads, in molded pieces, or as armature in sculptural or structural work. Don't forget that it is ideal for extending and expanding clay sheets and veneers, making your clay endeavors that much more affordable.

Scrap clay can be used as the foundation for foiled borders. However, it can be difficult, if not impossible, to adhere foil to round or rolled clay surfaces. The trick to using foil or leafing with clay is to create very thin veneers using the smallest settings of the pasta machine to create the foiled sheet that will be visible.

1 Apply the selected surface treatment as instructed to these thin sheets and attach to the junk clay base of your project.

2 Roll a junk clay snake to press into a border mold. The snake is laid over the thin, foiled clay strip and pressed into the mold cavity. Since the back of the border won't be visible, scrap is the ideal application for creating accents like these.

3 The excess clay is shaved from the flat surface of the mold.

4 The clay is gently eased out of the mold by the tail ends. Typically, foil, leaf, or embossing powder applied to polymer clay before molding or stamping acts as a resist agent when releasing the clay **a**. The results can be quite striking **b**.

4b

Additional Thoughts on Molding

Here, mica pigment powder is applied to the entire surface of clay shaped for pressing into a mold made from scrap clay and a metal stamping.

1 It's recommended that you mix scrap clay until it is a solid color when creating molds. This makes it easier to see if you have filled the mold properly.

2 This shows the different effects achieved when clay is molded using (top left to right) mica powder applied over the entire clay surface before molding, mica powder applied to the raised surface after molding, leaf applied before molding, and foil applied before molding.

Metal stampings can be used as molds. Unlike polymer clay molds, the clay can be baked inside. Many of the stampings in my collection are vintage and one-of-a-kind. I like to make duplicates using scrap clay so that I don't risk damaging the original, and this allows me to make several for use in workshops.

3 Just as antiquing stamped clay can offer strikingly bold visual results, the same can be said of antiquing molded clay. Here Rub 'n Buff®, a wax-based patina that comes in 20 colors and finishes,

is buffed onto the raised surface of these baked molded-clay pieces. These were made using a glass intaglio, which is quite small. The treatment highlights the fine details of the pieces.

The molded face in the photo at right is yet another example of how antiquing faux ivory brings out the realistic qualities of the technique | see FAUX IVORY, chapter 9, page 106 |.

TECHNIQUE #3
Leafing Pens

These markers come in metallic colors and deliver an opaque paint that is compatible with baked clay. These, along with permanent marking pens, are ideal for accenting or finishing edges on polymer clay work (see the photo below).

TECHNIQUE #4
Suspending Clay

The method for nontwist suspension is a sandwich process for embedding wire, eye pins, or head pins inside of clay assemblies for the purpose of hanging. This technique eliminates the need for making stringing channels prior to curing or drilling through thin layers of clay after baking. Instructions for this technique can be found in | HOLLOW FORMS, chapter 11, page 130 | and | SUSPENDED CRYSTAL PENDANT, chapter 14, page 160 |.

TECHNIQUE #5
Tube Attachments

Flat coil or clay sheets can be formed around a metal mandrel (knitting needle) and baked prior to attachment to a polymer clay focal piece. This becomes the means of stringing or suspending the clay (see the photos below and on the facing page).

The size of the mandrel (do not use wood) determines the size of the hole opening. For larger cording, use larger mandrels. The thickness of the clay sheeting used (or diameter of the clay snake) determines not only the outer finished diameter, but also the strength of the tube.

Thick to medium-thick clay sheets are recommended for most tube bails. Clay snake diameters from $1/16$ in. to $1/8$ in. are suggested, but don't hesitate to create larger or smaller diameter tubes or coils depending on your needs.

1 When creating tubes, cut the sheet edges at 45-degree angles so they abut more cleanly around the mandrel.

2 Roll the sheet around the mandrel and roll lightly over the work tile to meld and blend the seam.

3 Trim the desired length of your tube(s) with a clay blade while on the mandrel.

4 Bake the tubes while suspended on a box or bead rack to prevent a flat side from forming.

5 When the clay is cool, it can be gently twisted on the mandrel to loosen; then slide it off.

6 Attach suspension tubes/coils to uncured clay with a dab of bonder glue.

7 When the glue has set, brush liquid clay on both sides of the attachment to strengthen the connection and bake for at least 25 minutes. For added strength, tiny snakes of clay can be added after baking between the attachment and the clay focal piece and rebaked.

coil tube tips

- Make sure the diameter of the snake is as uniform as possible.

- Coil the clay tightly so that no gaps appear.

- Heat-set coils for 10 minutes on a suspended mandrel.

- After the coil has cooled from heat-setting, brush liquid clay all around and into the crevices to strengthen the coil (see the photo below). Bake again for 25 minutes.

- Make the coil longer than needed. Trim it to the desired size after baking.

Fold-Over Bails

Straight or angled strips of clay can be glued to the front and back of a clay focal piece as a suspension method. The strip is folded over a bakeable mandrel to hold the bail open and define the shape. The clay should be fairly thick to ensure finished strength. Again, as with tube/coil connections, the diameter of the mandrel will determine the size of your bail opening.

After baking and cooling, the mandrel is gently twisted to loosen and then pulled free from the clay.

Have fun creating a variety of fold-over bails. They can be simple or ornate and kept matte or polished smooth. Try adding decorative flair with foils, crystals, or other embellishments.

Findings

A variety of pin or bail attachments can be found in craft and bead stores for attaching to clay. These should not only be glued to the clay, but also anchored to your piece with some overlaid clay and baked again (see the left photo below).

Jewelry Basics

Making basic jewelry is a skill set that everyone who creates should have, even if you don't create jewelry with clay. You may find that these concepts will lend themselves to other ways of adding embellishment to your work. These techniques come easily with a little bit of practice. I suggest you start working with inexpensive wire and components until you feel comfortable with the concepts.

While having the best tools isn't absolutely necessary, it's not wise to scrimp too much on these. The old adage "you get what you pay for" is never truer than with jewelry tools. Good tools should have a comfortable grip, uniform jaws, and close fittings when closed.

It's a good idea to have separate cutters for fine- and heavier-gauge wires. Nippers meant for delicate wirework can

be easily damaged when cutting heavier gauges of wire. Most high-quality tools will last you a lifetime if used and stored properly, but cutters need to be changed from time to time. While the edges can be sharpened, this can be tricky. If notching appears in the blade edge, it's time to get new cutters.

It's also a good idea to get a wire gauge to determine the size of unidentified wire. The larger the gauge, the finer the wire. For example, while 16-gauge wire is a small number as gauges go, the wire itself is quite large in diameter and strong. On the other hand, 32-gauge wire is very fine and has the consistency of coarse hair (see the bottom right photo on the facing page).

Wire is also designated by hardnesses of dead soft (the softest), half-hard, or hard. Hammering or pulling through a drawplate can harden softer wire. Annealing (heating) can soften hard wire. Consult metal jewelry-making books and resources for more information on these concepts.

Working with Jump Rings

Jump rings are the tiny metal loops that are used as connectors in jewelry making.

The proper way to open and close a jump ring is to twist the ends apart on the same plane using two grooveless pairs of pliers.

Do not open by pulling the ends apart. This will not only distort the shape of the jump ring, but weaken the metal as well.

A tight, nearly invisible closure is always desired when working with jump rings. When twisting the ends of the ring back toward one another, apply a little inward pressure so that the opening overlaps slightly. This will put some tension in the wire.

Gently draw back one end with pliers and pull parallel with the other end until the ends are directly across from one another. You may even feel the wire "click" into place. Wire has a memory, and the tension caused by "overclosing" will help hold the jump ring tightly closed. Be sure to check the position of the ends both from the front and the top to make sure they are properly aligned.

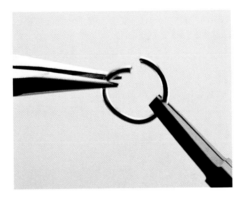

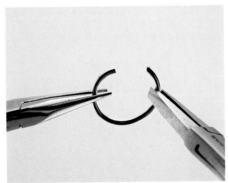

Forming an Eye Pin

Eye pins can be purchased, but they are very easy to make. Half-hard wire is typically the best to work with for making eye pins. The desired gauge depends on how strong the wire end needs to be.

For a standard loop, bend the wire back at a 90-degree angle using pliers. Trim the length of the wire to ¼ in. long for a very small loop, ⅜ in. long for an average loop, or ½ in. long for a large loop.

You may wish to suspend your piece without the use of a jump ring. If so, the bend should be made from front to back so the "eye" or loop appears invisible from the front of whatever you are suspending. This often means making a larger loop in order to pass a chain or cord through.

Connecting Pieces to Jump Rings

If you wish to connect your crystal, bead, or clay piece using a jump ring, you should bend the wire to the right or left side, parallel with the plane of your piece so that the loop or eye appears open from the front.

1 Once the wire is bent at 90 degrees and trimmed to the desired length, grasp the wire end between the jaws of round-nose pliers. The place at which you grasp the wire when forming the loop is important. The point you are starting from should be the same distance inward from the tips of the pliers as the length of the wire you are bending. For instance, if you are making an eye using a bent section trimmed to ⅜ in. long, you should grasp the wire end between the pliers' jaws ⅜ in. in from the end of the pliers' tip.

2 While holding the wire firmly, rotate the pliers one-half turn. Remove the pliers, reposition them and your hand, and complete the loop with a second half-turn.

3 The example at left in the photo below shows a properly formed eye pin. It should look like a balloon floating on a string. The example on the right is incorrectly formed. This was caused by not bending the wire at 90 degrees before turning around the jaw of the round-nose pliers.

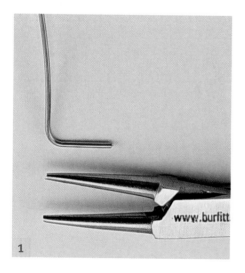

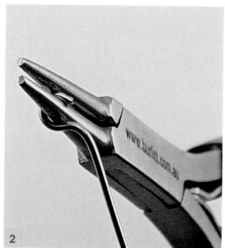

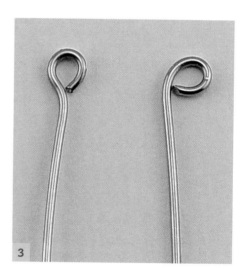

Fancy or Coil-Wrapped Loops

A fancy or coiled wrap makes the most secure loop possible without soldering. It also provides an elegant decorative finish to your hand-connected components.

1 When forming a coiled loop on wire coming out of clay or a bead, grasp the wire firmly at the end of the clay or bead. This length (approximately ⅛ in.) becomes the stem around which the wire is wrapped. Bend the wire above the plier jaw at a 90 degree angle. An ideal coil will wrap around one-and-a-half to three times before needing to be cut. Do not make the coil too long, as this can create a weak spot in your wire. Longer formations are more prone to bending. Repeated bending will work-harden the wire, making it brittle.

2 Rotate the pliers upward with a quarter turn of your wrist. Pull the wire end up, around, and over the top jaw of the pliers to form a hook-shaped partial loop.

Remember the point at which you grasp and wrap the wire between the jaws, as it will determine the size of your finished loop. Since round-nose pliers are tapered, the farther away from the tips you grasp the wire to make your loop, the larger it will be. The loop should now look like a shepherd's crook.

3 Rotate the pliers one half turn with your wrist, so that the bottom jaw is now on the top. Wrap the wire around the jaw that is now on the bottom. This will complete the loop. Hold the wire steady with the pliers in the loop.

4 Using your hands or another pair of pliers, wrap the wire end around the stem formed in Step 1. You will be able to make one-and-a-half to three rotations around the wire stem. Make rotations nice and tight.

Gaps in coils are unsightly. When you have wrapped as far as you can, pull the wire out slightly and cut on a diagonal using wire cutters. Use fine-tip pliers to bend or tuck the end in against the stem as far as possible. File the end if it is still rough to the touch.

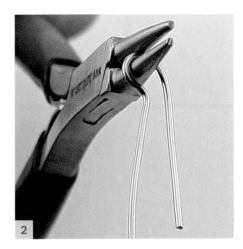

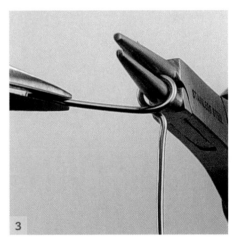

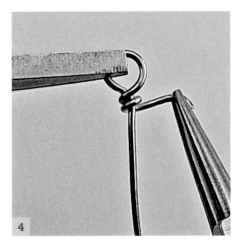

CHAPTER FOURTEEN

Projects to Make

IN THIS CHAPTER, YOU WILL FIND SIX PROJECTS of varying degrees of complexity and challenge. My wish is that you find one or more of them intriguing enough to try your hand at. I've attempted to include ideas that can be used a number of ways.

For instance, the concepts used in the Sutton Slice "About Face" Case can be applied to a variety of projects, including the embellishment of journal covers, boxes, and such. Also, consider the many options at hand for altering the finished look of these or any works you create, whether a change in color palette, pattern, or surface technique.

The important thing is to find your own creative "voice" as you enjoy the process, but remember that imitation is a wonderful way to hone your skills as you progress toward artistic mastery. Most of all, remember this is about getting in touch with your inner artist and having fun!

PROJECTS

- Suspended Crystal Pendant

- Magic Mirror: Millefiori-Tiled Surfaces Using Cane Remnants

- Swirly Whirly Faux Art Glass Bracelet

- Faux Dichroic Shield Pendant

- Image Transfer Inro Amulet

- Sutton Slice "About Face" Case

Suspended Crystal Pendant

MATERIALS NEEDED

Polymer clay in Raspberry, White, and Black

Clay-dedicated pasta machine

2 clay blades

Ball-tip stylus

Symmetrical/oblong canapé cutter (oval, football/marquis, or diamond shape)

1 CRYSTALLIZED–*Swarovski Elements* 21-mm by 7-mm Princess Baguette, Tanzanite

4-in. by 4-in. smooth ceramic work/ baking tile

Craft knife

Large knitting needle

Eye pin

Flat-nose pliers

28-gauge silver wire

22-gauge silver wire

Two-part, five-minute setting epoxy

Lisa Pavelka Poly Bonder glue

Acrylic roller

Coffee straw

2 CRYSTALLIZED–*Swarovski Elements* Swarovski PP18 Crystal Chatons

Coarse sandpaper

CREATE AN EDGY LOOK WITH A GRADIENT BACKGROUND that showcases a focal crystal stone and a unique wire accent. Consider making varied versions of this concept using different shaped cutters and crystals.

1 Make a Skinner Blend from White to Raspberry, and reduce it to 1 in. in diameter. Cut a ⅛-in.-think slice from the cane and roll through the third-largest setting of the pasta machine. Stipple the surface with a ball-tip stylus.

2 Press the baguette stone into the center of the clay to create a depression setting. Center the cutter over the clay and cut out the shape, removing the excess clay.

3 Mark notches along the sides of the piece using the tip of the knitting needle. This marks the placement of the wire coils being added in later steps. There should be a total of four notches, as shown. Make the marks approximately one-third of the way down from the top and bottom ends of the crystal.

Bake the piece for 10 to 15 minutes in a preheated oven at the recommended temperature (use a thermometer) for 10 minutes.

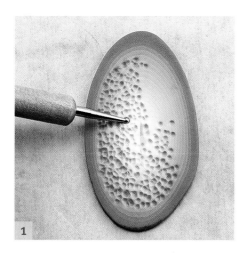

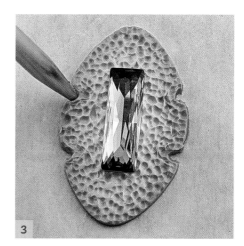

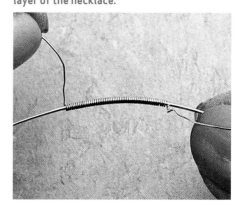

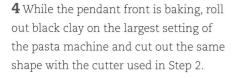

4 While the pendant front is baking, roll out black clay on the largest setting of the pasta machine and cut out the same shape with the cutter used in Step 2.

5 To create the suspension wire, hold an eye pin with the hole facing away from you. Make wavy bends in the pin wire. Press the bent length into the top of the black clay cutout with the eye of the pin overhanging the edge. Leave ⅛ in. of the suspension wire under the "eye" extended beyond the clay's edge. This is where the striped border will fit in a later step. Make sure the wire is pressed all the way into the clay so it lies flush with the surface.

6 Coil the 28-gauge wire around two 2-in.-long pieces of 22-gauge wire. Each coil length should measure about ¾ in.; it should be long enough to cover the crystal and most of the clay width.

7 When the top piece of the pendant has cooled, gently pry the crystal loose and reattach it using the epoxy. When the glue has set, wrap the wire coils over the

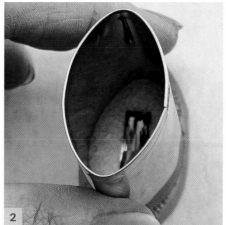

crystal and bend the ends around the edges, along the notches made in Step 3. Fold the wire ends flat against the back of the clay. Apply clay bonder glue over the back of the pendant's top and press firmly into the black clay base.

Trim excess black clay with the craft knife. Bake the piece again for 10 minutes.

note

Do not cut the 22-gauge wire that the thinner wire is wrapped around. This excess length will be used to wrap around the top layer of the necklace.

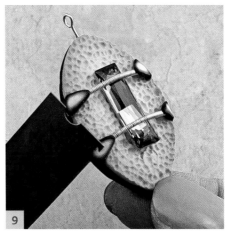

tip

When adding the crystals in step 13, make a small hole in the center first, using a needle tool or toothpick to create a recess where the crystal can be more easily seated in the clay. Crystals should be pressed deeply enough so that the clay rises up and over the edge to form a natural bezel edge. Bake the pendant one last time for 30 minutes.

8 Roll a small section of a black-to-white Skinner Blend bull's-eye cane to ¼ in. in diameter. Pinch into a teardrop shape and cut four slices from the cane (flip the cane over after each slice to help maintain the teardrop shape). Glue these with the tips facing inward over the sides of the pendant to conceal and embellish the wires along the edges.

9 Trim any overhanging clay from the teardrops away from the pendant's edge using the clay blade.

10 While the clay is baking, make a black-and-white-striped loaf by stacking two 2-in. by 2-in. sheets of clay over one another. Run these combined sheets through the largest setting of the pasta machine. Cut in quarters and stack with alternating strips. Cut this stack in half and restack.

11 Cut two slices from the stack with a sharp, clean clay blade. Lay each slice (with stripes alternating) over a thin

strip of black clay rolled out on the fifth-largest setting of the pasta machine. Roll the striped strip through the second-largest setting of the pasta machine with the stripes facing up (vertically). Trim the uneven edges and cut the strip in half lengthwise to create two striped strips.

12 When the pendant has cooled, glue the strips on either side with clay bonder. Trim excess clay from the top and bottom surfaces with the clay blade.

13 Punch out two small circles of black clay from a sheet rolled through the largest setting of the pasta machine using a 1-in.-long piece cut from a coffee straw. Apply each ball to the top and bottom sections of the pendant using bonder glue, pressing slightly flat with your fingertip. Place a chaton crystal over the center of each ball and press into the clay.

Finishing the Piece

The personal philosophy that I share with all my students is that the difference between an artist and a crafter is the quality of your finishing. Even if no one ever sees the back of your work besides you, you'll achieve greater satisfaction from your creative effects if you finish all aspects of your work. I finish the back of most jewelry pieces by gluing a thin layer of black clay over the back (run through the fifth- or sixth-largest setting of a pasta machine).

I texture this piece to hide any marring, fingerprints, or nicks and to give it some character. Stipple with a stylus or press a texture sheet or coarse sandpaper over the clay. Trim the excess clay after texturing. Rebake the piece for 15 minutes.

Another advantage to applying a clay layer to the backing is that it will camouflage any gaps or distorted edges or borders that may have been added to your work. I even add black clay to sterling and fine silver settings to prevent the black tarnish marks that can be left against skin while being worn.

I don't recommend using other colors or cane slices since they will become discolored over time due to rubbing against skin or fabric. Black will always remain clean looking.

Notice the difference an added backing can make to the finished quality of this piece.

Magic Mirror: Millefiori-Tiled Surfaces Using Cane Remnants

MATERIALS NEEDED

3 to 5 cane ends, 1 in. long

Clay blade

Acrylic roller

Craft knife

Clay-dedicated pasta machine

Lisa Pavelka Poly Bonder glue

Pillbox or other small tin

1 CRYSTALLIZED–*Swarovski Elements* Flatback 10SS Crystal

Tweezers

Needle tool or coffee stirrer

IT'S EASY TO CREATE A VARIETY OF COMPLEX CANES using cane remnants from other projects. There are endless possibilities for intricate patterns using a few simple manipulations or random assemblies. This project uses cane slices to cover a pillbox. You can make quick and easy treasure cases using all types of containers.

One of my favorites is empty candy and mint tins, but don't stop there! Create tiled cane veneers for projects and surfaces including light-switch plates, jewelry settings, beads, and more.

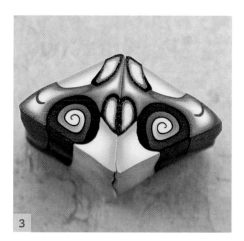

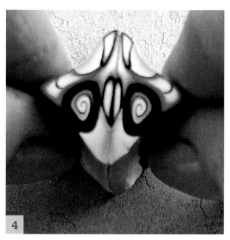

1 Assemble the cane ends in any random fashion. Note how the pink and white Skinner Blend cane was cut into sections. You'll get interesting pattern variations by cutting and/or reshaping the cane ends you select.

Make sure the cane ends you choose to create the mirror cane have significant contrast from light to dark colors between them.

Also avoid using too many cane ends or those that have very busy patterns. Too many fine details or lack of contrast can result in finished canes that are indistinct or muddied in appearance.

2 Compress the canes together and form into a triangular shape. Refine with your fingers as you squeeze and stretch during the compression/reduction process. For cane reduction tips | see CANE REDUCTION, chapter 4, page 49 |. Reduce and elongate to 4 in.

3 Cut off the distorted ends and assemble the ends together with two sides mirroring one another. Just as with Kaleidoscope Caning, the sides you mirror will determine the type of pattern that is created. Making canes using larger components will allow you to create multiple variations of the same cane and explore a multitude of patterns that can be made from the same components.

4 The cane assembly will now have a diamond shape. Compress the elongated ends in toward one another using your fingers as shown to create a square shape.

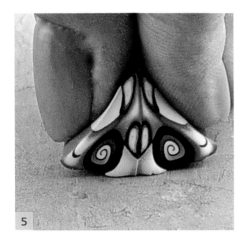

5

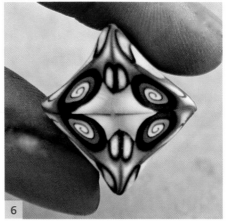

6

7

tip

Using a roller is preferred over a pasta machine to smooth and flatten millefiori veneers, as it is easier to prevent distortion while the clay stretches. The pasta machine does not allow for controlled stretching.

5 Flatten the square cane on one side and reshape and compress the entire length into a triangle cane again. As with Step 3, the side that is triangulated will affect the type of pattern that is created. There is no right or wrong side to select. This is one of the more playful aspects of working with polymer clay: Whichever one you choose will result in an exciting pattern. The mystery lies in what will be revealed by the direction you choose.

6 Cut the cane in half and assemble again with two sides mirroring one another as in Step 3.

7 Use your fingers and the acrylic roller to reduce the cane and refine it into a crisp square about 4½ in. long. Cut off the distorted ends and cut the length

into quarters. Assemble the quarters into a square cane that allows four identical sides to mirror one another. Here are two variations made by mirroring different corners in at the center.

8 Cut four thin slices (¹⁄₁₆ in. thick) and lay them over a piece of white clay, rolled through the fifth-largest setting of the pasta machine. The edges of these slices should also mirror one another and be butted up against one another as closely as possible. Roll the slices together to meld them using the acrylic roller.

9 Glue to the surface of the pillbox using clay bonder. Trim the excess clay from the edges with the craft knife. Bake the box at the recommended temperature for 10 minutes to set the clay.

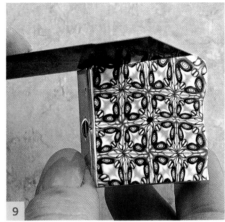

9

VARIATION

Sometimes the center corners of tiled cane slices don't meet up as cleanly as you might like, or the stretching process creates significant distortion of the pattern in the middle. Adding a flatback crystal pressed into a tiny ball of clay where these corners meet is not only a nice way to accent your work, but it also works to camouflage these areas.

10 Roll out black clay (or another complementary clay color) on the fourth-largest setting of the pasta machine. Cut the clay into four strips slightly wider and longer than each side of the container you are covering. Glue these to the sides one at a time with bonder glue and trim the edges with the clay blade.

11 Texture the sides of the box for a more finished appearance. I used a technique I call "creping" on the edge. To create the look of creped fabric, press a needle tool or coffee stirrer vertically into the clay repeatedly. Retrim to remove any clay that spreads out over the edges during texturing. Bake the box one final time for 25 minutes.

10

11

Swirly Whirly Faux Art Glass Bracelet

MATERIALS NEEDED

Polymer clay in Sahara, Sunflower Yellow, Copper, Mandarin Orange, White, Black, and Caramel

Acrylic roller

Clay-dedicated pasta machine

Clay blade

Very coarse sandpaper

Lisa Pavelka Oval Bracelet Finding

Large Kemper Oval Clay Cutter

Emery file

Lisa Pavelka Poly Bonder glue

Toothpick

Small butane torch (or other direct heat source)

Optional: UV cure lamp

Two-part, five-minute setting epoxy

USE A MIRRORED GRADIENT LOAF TO CREATE FINE STRIPS, which are formed into whimsical swirls. This is the basis for a panel bracelet that looks amazingly like blown art glass. This deceptively simple project is the ideal activity for an afternoon or evening of creative fun, whether you're making a single project for yourself, for a gift, or to sell.

The bracelet finding can be separated for use as single- or multiple-panel pendants or as earring backings. UV resin adds the pièce de résistance that gives the amazingly realistic look of glass.

ISOSCELES TRIANGLE   RIGHT TRIANGLE

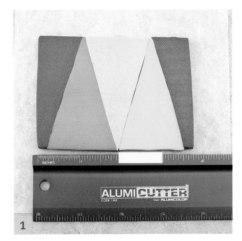

1 Create five different-colored triangles using any clay colors except White and Black. Three of the triangles should be isosceles triangles and two should be right triangles with a blunted tip. When preparing the clay for the templates, roll out each color on the largest setting of the pasta machine and stack double layers for each color. Turn the sheet into a gradient loaf | see GRADIENT LOAVES, chapter 3, page 43 |.

2 Make an accordion-folded loaf from the sheets following the directions for this technique (also on page 43).

3 Compress the loaf slightly to compact it using your hand or a few firm passes with an acrylic roller. Cut the loaf in half through the middle and stack with two identical colors mirroring one another. Recompress these together once again as before.

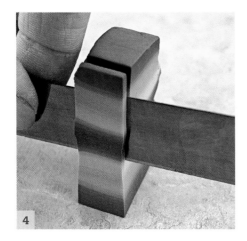

4 Cut a ⅛-in.-thick slice.

5 Roll this through the largest setting of the pasta machine with the stripes facing vertically, or upward.

6 Turn the slice so the stripes are facing horizontally and thin it by passing it through the second-largest setting of the pasta machine. Repeat this, passing the strip in the same direction through the third- to sixth-largest settings of the pasta machine.

7 Make six 1-in. by 1-in. black clay squares from a sheet rolled through the fifth-largest setting of the pasta machine. Cut six thin, tapered strips of clay from the gradient sheet. Apply each strip to the clay squares by pressing the narrow end of a strip down over the center of the black clay to secure the tip. Coil the strip around to form a gradient swirl. Make sure that there is black clay showing through the rotations.

8 Press the sandpaper down repeatedly over the raised coils to texture. Do not use too much pressure while texturing to avoid overflattening the clay swirls. Cut out the ovals with the clay cutter. Bake the ovals for 20 minutes in a preheated oven at the recommended temperature. If needed, smooth the edges of the baked ovals with an emery file after baking.

9 Pour a thick dollop of Lisa Pavelka Poly Bonder glue on the center of the cooled clay ovals and spread out toward the edges using a needle tool or toothpick. Remove air bubbles by passing a direct heat source over the poly bonder glue for a few seconds and cure outdoors in direct sunlight or under a UV cure lamp for 10 to 15 minutes, following product directions. When the poly bonder glue is cured, glue the clay ovals to the bracelet finding with epoxy.

PROJECT

Faux Dichroic Shield Pendant

MATERIALS NEEDED

Polymer clay in Black

Craft knife

Scrap paper or cookie cutter

Clay-dedicated pasta machine

Lisa Pavelka Clay Foil in Rainbow

Lisa Pavelka Crackle Texture Stamp

Flexible clay blade

Permanent markers in various colors

10-mm jump ring

Three 8-mm jump rings

Lisa Pavelka Magic-Glos

Toothpick

Small butane torch (or other direct heat source)

Scrap paper

Optional: UV cure lamp, CRYSTALLIZED–
  Swarovski Elements Pointed Back
  Chaton Crystal

Lisa Pavelka Poly Bonder glue

DICHROIC GLASS IS EXCEPTIONALLY STRIKING, BUT IT CAN BE QUITE COSTLY. Working with glass requires sophisticated and expensive tools and is very labor intensive. You can get the look of this beautiful medium quite easily using a polymer clay base, clay foils, and UV resin.

Since there is no waste with foil, just as with clay, this is the ideal project for using up scrappy bits of foil from previous projects. I call this type of application "confetti foiling." It can be a lot of fun trying this concept with different colors of foil, and various sizes and shapes for the finished pieces.

No bezel setting is required to create this project, and a hidden suspension method offers a clean, modern appearance for hanging the pendant when finished.

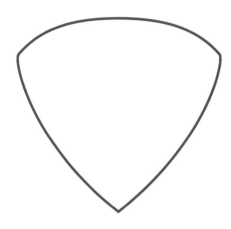

1 Trace the bowed triangle pattern or create a pattern of your own on scrap paper. (Alternative methods for creating the finished shape of the piece include using freehand cutting or using a cookie cutter.)

2 Roll out a 2½-in. by 2½-in. sheet of black clay on the third-largest setting of the pasta machine. The adhesion method for the foil differs somewhat from the technique for applying larger sections to polymer clay | see LEAF AND FOILING EFFECTS, chapter 8, page 90 |. Hold your fingertip down over the foil to heat it or burnish a small area for a few seconds to apply a small, irregular piece of foil. Continue to do this with the colors of your choice until you are satisfied with the pattern. You may wish to cover all the exposed black clay or leave some of the black peeking through for added contrast (as with the sample piece).

3 Press the texture stamp down over the foiled clay. The goal isn't necessarily to get a specific or repeating pattern with this project, but that is another option available to you. The method is simply to intensify the refractive properties of the foil. Texture repositions small areas of the surface so that it reflects and refracts light and color when seen at various angles.

4 Lay the template over the foiled clay and cut out the shape with the clay blade (or use one of the other shaping options mentioned in Step 1). Bake the clay for 10 minutes at the recommended temperature.

5 Roll out black clay through the second-largest setting of the pasta machine. Use the template to cut out the identical shape made in the last step.

OPTIONAL

If the foil colors fade when baked (see chapter 8 for details), you can touch up the color using brightly colored and fluorescent permanent markers. Rebake the clay for a few minutes to set the ink.

6 Press the 10-mm jump ring (with the opening facing inward) down into the top center of the black clay backing. The ring should be pressed deeply enough to lie flush with the surface of the black clay. Make sure that enough open area is exposed over the edge in order to add one or more jump rings after finishing the pendant for suspension on a cord or chain. Firmly press the baked pendant onto the black backing using bonder glue.

7 Trim the excess clay by gliding the craft knife around the pendant edges. Rebake the pendant for 20 minutes.

8 When the clay has cooled, add a thick layer of resin to the surface, applying it in the middle and spreading it outward with the toothpick. Remove air bubbles by passing a direct heat source over the resin for a few seconds and cure in direct sunlight or under a UV lamp for 10 to 15 minutes, following product directions.

9 Hang on a cord or chain with the three 8-mm jump rings.

OPTIONAL

Drill a conical hole into the cured resin using a pointed carbide drill bit in a rotary tool. Glue in a pointed-back crystal using jewelry cement.

> *note*
>
> **Larger pieces of clay and those without bezel edges or side walls may require an additional layer or two of resin (curing between layers) in order for the product to fill out all the way to the edges. The more layers that are added, the more rounded the surface of the piece will be.**

Image Transfer Inro Amulet

MATERIALS NEEDED

Polymer Clay in Black, Metallic Pearl, Sunflower Yellow, Caramel, and Metallic Gold

Clay-dedicated pasta machine

Pearl Ex mica powder in Gold

Lisa Pavelka Crackle Texture Stamp

Flexible clay blade

Deli paper

Small glass or metal bottle with $1\frac{1}{2}$-in diameter

Lisa Pavelka Waterslide Transfers

Lisa Pavelka Poly Bonder glue

Large knitting needle

Liquid polymer clay

1 pearl (mine was approx. $\frac{1}{4}$ in. by $\frac{1}{2}$ in.)

Gold metallic leafing

Craft knife

Automotive protectant spray

Lisa Pavelka Ropes & Braids Border Mold

Coarse sandpaper

Hand or rotary drill with graduated bits

Gold rattail cording

Large-holed brass bead

8-mm gold jump ring

Optional: Small gold tassel

Inros are a Japanese art form consisting of small singular or stacked boxes with a sliding lid. They originated as a means to hold personal objects such as cosmetics, medicinal herbs, needles, or perfume. These were suspended from obi sashes worn with kimonos, as these garments didn't have pockets.

Craftsmen made them from ivory (bone), wood, or lacquerware. Inros are a wonderful adornment to wear as a functional necklace. I like to wear mine at trade shows to hold money or as a way of delivering aromatherapy with a perfumed cotton ball inside.

Traditional inros can be round, oval, or sculptural, but they typically have dimension all around. The concept here is a twist on traditional shapes. The flat backing allows the inro to lie more comfortably against the neckline or breastbone. Once you are familiar with this construction concept, think of the different shaped forms (such as canapé cutters) that can be used to create a variety of unique inro amulets.

1 Roll out a 2½-in. by 3½-in. sheet of black clay on the second-largest setting of the pasta machine. Apply gold mica powder to the surface of a clean, dry rubber texture stamp using your index finger.

2 Lay the black clay over the powdered stamp and lightly burnish with your fingers to transfer the powder pattern to the clay. Carefully lift the clay from the stamp to avoid smearing the pattern.

3 Trim the clay to 2 in. by 3 in. Cover the clay with a piece of deli paper to protect the powder. Lay it over the bottle with the longer side going around the circumference.

4 Roll out a piece of Metallic Pearl clay on the fifth-largest setting of the pasta machine. Apply a preprinted or custom inkjet waterslide transfer to the clay following the product directions. Trim around the image, leaving a ⅛-in.-wide border on all sides. Apply a little glue to the back of the pearl clay and lay it over the black, patterned clay.

tip

Be sure to tap off any excess mica powder after each dip into the jar to prevent powder clumps from contaminating the stamp recesses.

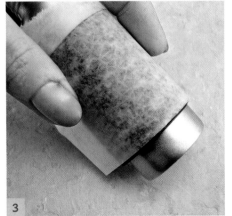

5

6

7a

7b

5 Determine whether you want the image centered or applied askew for a more artful feel. Gently smooth the edges to ensure they make contact with the black clay. Drag down the edges of the pearl clay onto the black clay beneath using the end of the knitting needle. This creates a bit of flattened deckle effect and secures the transfer clay to the inro base. Rub a thin layer of liquid clay over the transfer to seal it.

6 Roll a small ball of Metallic Gold clay into an elongated oval. Flatten slightly with your fingers and glue to one corner of the transfer with clay bonder. Apply a little bonder to the back of the pearl and press into the Metallic Gold clay. Smooth and press the edges of the gold clay up and around the pearl to create a bit of a bezel that secures it in place.

7 Make a simple Skinner-Blended bull's-eye leaf cane | see SKINNER BLENDING, chapter 3, page 36 | **a**. Compress and reduce the cane to ¼ in. in diameter; shape and slice the cane following the directions in | MILLEFIORI CANING, chapter 4, pages 48–52 | **b**.

8 Cut several dozen slices. Place the slices over the inro front in any patterns or formations that you find pleasing. Bake the clay while on the bottle at the recommended temperature for 15 minutes.

9 Add gold leaf to a 2-in. by 2-in. piece of black clay. Roll the clay through the second-largest setting of the pasta machine. Fold the clay in half and pass through the second-largest setting again. Gently pry the cooled clay from the bottle. Apply a thin line of glue on both exposed edges of the inro cover. Press down firmly over the leafed clay. With the piece lying flat, trim the excess clay from all four edges using the clay blade. Bake while flat for 10 minutes.

10 Apply bonder glue to the bottom of the cooled inro front and press down into a 1½-in. by 2½-in. piece of gold clay rolled through the largest setting of the pasta machine. Trim the excess clay from around the front and back with the craft knife so that the gold bottom conforms only to the edges of the inro form. Poke two holes about 1 in. apart through the bottom of the inro using the tip of the knitting needle. Don't worry about the size of the holes at this point. They will be drilled open in a later step. Rebake for 10 minutes.

tips

• Try your hand at adding dimension to your slices by gently twisting the ends or raising the edges using the needle tool.

• It may be helpful to apply tiny dots of bonding glue before adding cane slices to help them adhere, since the mica powder can act as a resist agent. Be sure to use bonder glue sparingly, as too much may extrude out when pressing slices into place. Visible glue may also discolor when baking. Remember, less is always more with glue!

• Use a piece of scrap clay to make a tiny trough to set the bottle on when baking to prevent it from rolling.

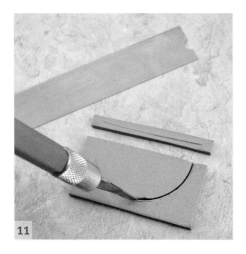

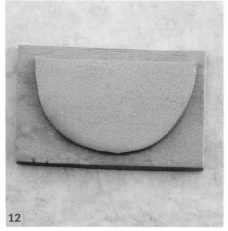

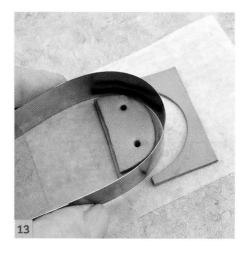

11 When the inro has cooled, press the open top down over a sheet of Metallic Gold clay that's been rolled through the largest setting of the pasta machine and remove. This will leave an outline in the clay. Cut along the inner edge of these lines to form the inside of the lid. After cutting, check to make sure the half circle you cut fits cleanly inside the inro opening.

12 Place this piece over another sheet of gold clay that's also been rolled through the largest setting of the pasta machine.

13 Rub a little automotive protectant spray along the edges of the sheet that surround the lid insert. Press the open end of the inro back down over the gold clay insert and onto the sheet using light pressure. This will leave another cutting outline.

Remove the inro body. Cut along the outside edge of the marked lines.

Mark holes in the lid with the knitting needle by referring to the spacing of the holes made in the inro bottom for placement. Bake the lid for 10 minutes at the recommended temperature.

tip

If you cannot find a bead that works, make one from clay. Use the knitting needle to make the holes to form your bead around to get the correct size. Finish off the ends with the jewelry findings of your choice. Or you might add a decorative tassel or other dangling embellishment at the bottom of the inro with a jump ring attached to the cording.

14 Make molded borders of gold clay with a thin rope design. Dust gold mica powder onto the raised area of the borders to highlight them. Attach borders around the top and bottom curves of the inro with bonder glue. Bake the inro and the lid for 10 minutes.

15 After the lid has cooled, roll gold clay through the sixth-largest setting of the pasta machine, glue this sheet to the top of the lid, and trim. Texture with coarse sandpaper and retrim. Bake the lid and the inro separately one last time for 25 minutes at the recommended temperature.

16 When the pieces have cooled, drill the holes open, starting with smaller bits and working your way up to larger bits that allow the threading of your chosen cording.

Thread the ends of the cording up through the bottom two holes of the inro and out through the two lid holes. Add the brass or other focal bead over the two cord ends. The hole of the bead should be large enough to allow both cords to pass through, but snug enough to not move freely unless pulled. This creates a friction clasp.

Sutton Slice "About Face" Case

MATERIALS NEEDED

Polymer Clay in Pearl, Raspberry, Pacific Blue, White, Emerald, Flesh Light, Gold, Caramel, Green, Metallic Sapphire Blue, and Pacific Blue

Acrylic roller

Ancient Page™ Dye Ink in Coal, or other black stamp ink

Lisa Pavelka About Face and Love Letter Texture Stamps

Lisa Pavelka Poly Bonder glue

Business card holder or small tin

Deli paper

2-in.-long plastic-coated magnet or dowel

Clay-dedicated pasta machine

Automotive protectant spray

Blush

Small paintbrush

Eye shadow

Craft knife

Clay blade

Needle tool

Liquid polymer clay

2 in. (19 stones) CRYSTALLIZED–*Swarovski Elements* Plastic Banded Trim #50-002

Ball-tip stylus

Coarse sandpaper

Wavy clay blade

CRYSTALLIZED–*Swarovski Elements* Flatback Hotfix Crystals

Lisa Pavelka Small and Medium Rose Leaf Embossing Cutters

Lisa Pavelka Polymer Clay Foil in silver

Packing tape

CRYSTALLIZED–*Swarovski Elements* Flatback 10-mm by 5-mm Rose Water Opal Navette

Fine-tip tweezers

By now you're probably familiar with the Sutton Slice technique | see BASIC SUTTON SLICE SHEET, chapter 10, page 115 |. The concept was introduced in chapter 10 with a basic two-tone method. A more intricate and challenging version of the technique lies in the use of multiple colored clays inserted in individual cavities of the texture stamp.

I designed a number of my texture stamps with this concept in mind. There are wide arrays of other texture stamps that work well with both the basic and advanced Sutton Slice techniques. I encourage anyone trying the project below to build his or her skill level with practice of the basic technique first.

I can't stress enough how important it is to use softer clay and a stamp that is very clean and dry in order for the technique to work well. Also, since all clays have a specific open time (a period of being conditioned and pliable), it is advisable to do this project in a single sitting.

A variety of clay techniques covered in this book lend themselves to the other elements of this project. I hope you'll agree that the combination of treatments makes for an elegant visual effect for this most practical of projects. While a business card case was used for this project, consider applying the concept to a variety of surfaces from jewelry to home décor items.

1 Roll out a sheet of pearl clay on the sixth-largest setting of the pasta machine. It should be slightly larger than the case being covered. Roll the clay once or twice with the acrylic roller to make sure there are no ripples in the surface. Stamp the clay with the inked Love Letter stamp and set aside to dry. Once dry, glue to the case using bonder glue.

note

The front edge of the case will need to be trimmed while faceup and with the lid open since this side is slightly shorter than the front of the base on the case.

tip

Cover the top with deli paper during this step to protect the stamped area from smudging.

Apply glue to one-third of the case at a time and lay the end of the clay down over the glued area. Smooth the clay onto the case's surface from one direction to the other while the deli paper is still in place. Lift the clay and continue to glue the stamped clay down over the second and last third of the case to prevent air pockets from forming while you attach the clay base.

Turn the case over with the deli paper still in place and trim the excess clay from the edges.

2 Start by pressing flesh-colored clay (or clay tinted with a tiny amount of other color for a variety of other skin tones) into the face and neck cavity. Follow the instructions and tips for the Sutton Slice method | see BASIC SUTTON SLICE SHEET, chapter 10, page 115 |. Next, add some color for the lips. I mixed a tiny amount of Raspberry and White clay together for this. Remove clay embedded in these areas with the craft knife.

For the hair, some Gold and Caramel clay was blended without mixing all the way. The flower centers were mostly white, blended with a tiny amount of raspberry. Raspberry clay was also used for the outside petals of the flowers. Emerald clay was pressed into the leaves.

2

note

Important! Always use a fresh piece of clay when starting to work with the second and additional colors. Failure to do this may contaminate the pattern from the front. When slicing the clay away, the blade picks up thin shavings of other colors in surrounding cavities. Using a fresh pinch of clay to fill empty cavities will ensure that other colors don't get mixed into the color you are using. Even when you use fresh pieces of clay when adding a secondary or other color, there will be some surface contamination, although this won't be visible from the front when the clay is released from the stamp.

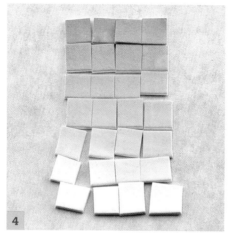

3 Once the face, leaves, and flower cavities have been filled, it's time to fill the background area. Mix one-quarter bar of white clay with a large pinch of both Pacific and Metallic Sapphire Blue clays. Roll this out on the largest setting and make a Skinner Blended sheet with white clay as the second color.

Use a plastic-coated magnet or wooden dowel placed on one end of the pasta machine to shorten the length of the rollers. This will limit the length the clay can stretch when being blended, making a narrow gradient sheet. This sheet should be the approximate size of the stamp area being filled (1¼ in. by 2¼ in.). If the sheet is much smaller, stretch it to size with a roller. Cut a ⅛-in.-wide strip from the length of the blended sheet and set it aside for later.

4 Cut the blended sheet into small squares with the clay blade.

5 Take a square from the lightest end of the sheet and press it into the background areas at the bottom of the face pattern. Continue to use squares from this first row to fill spaces and slice the background clay away until you have reached the other side of the face. Remember to use a fresh piece of clay each time you fill the next cavity area.

Continue to work your way upward, filling the background with darker and darker rows of clay squares until you have filled the entire background. Double-check the stamp to make sure all areas have been filled and there is no visible clay on the surface of the rubber **a**.

Note the color contamination that is visible on the surface of the stamp. This won't show when the clay is released onto the substrate layer of black clay **b**.

6 Check to make sure that every shaving and piece of scrap clay is removed from the stamp and work area. Roll out a 2-in. by 3-in. sheet of black clay on the fourth-largest setting of the pasta machine. Place the sheet facedown over the clay-

5b

6

7

8

9

embedded stamp. Apply a small amount of automotive protectant spray to your fingers and tap them over the surface of the black clay very firmly for a minute or two. Use a lot of pressure and force as you tap. The goal is for the substrate layer of black clay to fuse with the clay inside the stamp.

Once you are sure that you have sufficiently pressed the black clay down all over, make one firm pass with the acrylic roller. Do not roll it back and forth.

7 Holding the stamp and clay in one hand, bend the edge of the stamp backward, almost folding it in half, and slowly roll the stamp off the clay. Do not pull the clay backing.

It's important to remove the stamp from the clay and not pull the clay off the stamp, which could leave areas of clay still embedded in the stamp. If this occurs | see TROUBLESHOOTING FOR POLYMER CLAY beginning on page 208 |.

8 Optional: Brush a little blush over the cheekbone of the face and dust the eyelid with some eye shadow. Be sure to clean the brush well between colors of makeup by stroking the brush several times over a clean rag.

9 Trim the excess black clay away from the side of the Sutton Slice face panel that will be facing inward on your case. Deckle (tear) this edge by pulling tiny bits of the black clay away with the tip of your craft knife.

10 Trim the black clay along the outer edge of the face panel to about ¼ in. wide. Apply a few strokes of bonder glue on the back of the black clay and attach the panel to the case. Press the panel down all around with light pressure. Trim the excess clay from the three sides of the case with the clay blade.

11 Make a trough along the exposed black clay edge on the outside of the face panel using the needle tool. Apply a bead of liquid clay in the trough and press a premeasured length of plastic banded crystals into to the depression. The liquid clay will flow over the connecting fiber of the banding and fuse it to the case while baking. It won't be visible after curing.

12 Use a ball-tip stylus to texture the black clay. This will also press the clay up and around the banding for added security.

13 Cut a ⅜-in.-wide strip of black clay from a sheet rolled out on the fifth-largest setting of the pasta machine. Texture it with sandpaper and then deckle one vertical edge. Glue this strip with the deckled edge facing inward on

the end opposite the face panel. Trim the excess clay from three sides with the clay blade.

Roll the gradient blend strip that was set aside in Step 3 very thin. Insert the strip with the gradient pattern lying horizontally along the rollers. Run it through gradually thinner settings, ending on the sixth-largest setting. Cut a tapered strip from this sheet with the wavy blade. Attach the strip to the textured black clay strip on the left as shown. Press flat-back crystals into the clay at the ends of the vine swirls of the face panel and at the narrow end of the gradient wavy strip.

14 Texture a small piece of black clay rolled through the sixth-largest setting of the pasta machine with sandpaper. Cut out a leaf (without embossing) using the

Medium Rose Leaf Embossing Cutter. Glue this to the center of the exposed letter-stamped clay at an angle. Cut a thin slice from a ½-in.-diameter Skinner Blended bull's-eye cane (Raspberry/White was used). The slice should be rolled through the fourth-largest setting of the pasta machine and needs to be slightly larger than the size of the small rose leaf cutter.

Apply Silver Foil to the slice | see APPLYING FOIL, chapter 8, page 94 |. Press the cutter down over the foiled clay and emboss by depressing the plunger down firmly. Lightly burnish packing tape over the leaf using the Pavelka Peel | see THE PAVELKA PEEL, chapter 8, page 98 | and repeat, leaving the foil recessed in the vein lines. Glue the leaf over the center of the black textured leaf.

15 Roll a small ball of black clay into an oval and glue at the wide end of the black leaf. Slightly flatten with your fingertip. Poke a hole in the center with the needle tool. Using fine-tip tweezers, press the navette crystal into the clay oval with the pointed end of the crystal inserted into the needle tool hole.

Roll a small snake of black clay and wrap it around the outside of the crystal starting from the side facing the leaf. This will form a bezel edge and secure the crystal in place. Blend the seam of the snake into the leaf using the tip of the craft knife. Bake card holder in a preheated oven at the recommended temperature for 30 minutes.

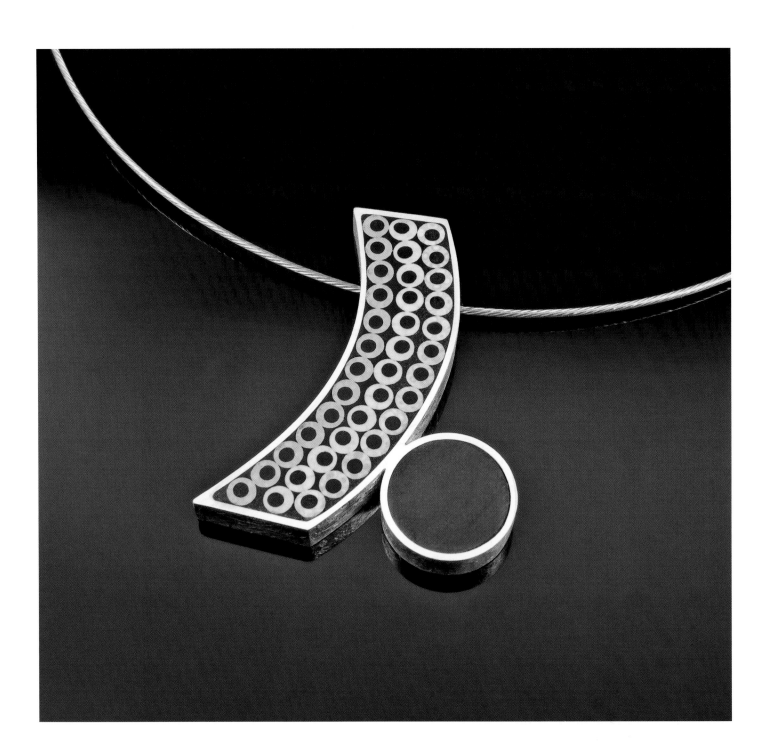

CHAPTER FIFTEEN

Gallery of Polymer Clay Art

MORE THAN TWO DECADES OF WORKING with polymer clay have provided me the privilege of developing deep friendships and acquaintances with a group of remarkably talented artists. This gallery showcases the work of just a handful of these incredibly gifted individuals, along with a few additional examples of my own efforts. These selections are offered to further inspire you with the potential of polymer clay as a creative medium.

The world is filled with countless clay aficionados, both professional and amateur, who continue to astound with their exceptional skill. I'm privileged to offer their creations as a representation of such talent. Each piece featured is an example of single or composite techniques explained in this book. Some works are exquisite in their simplicity, while others amaze with their precision and complexity.

I greatly appreciate the generosity of these artists for sharing their artwork. I hope you find this section a further source of encouragement for achieving your own polymer clay masterworks. The artists featured signify a group of established professionals known throughout the world for their skills, as well as up-and-coming designers who are sure to become increasingly influential in the creative arts.

△ *On the Canal* by Sarah Shriver
Millefiori caning and polishing techniques (1$^1/_2$ in. by 1$^1/_2$ in.).

◁ *Untitled* by Bettina Welker
Fabricated sterling silver bezel filled with polymer clay inlay (1$^1/_2$ in. by 2 in. by $^1/_8$ in.).

▷ *Game of Black and White* by Nevenka Sabo
Simple caning in black and white combined to make motif applied over plain ceramic tile (6 in. by 6 in.).

△ *Pansy Garden* by Toni M. Ransfield
Chicken egg layered with base of pink metallic clay and thinly sliced millefiori canes, then sanded and buffed to high shine (3 in. by 1 in.).

▷ *Faux Porcelain Beads* by Deborah Anderson
Image transfer onto clay with translucent clay on top; hollow beads assembled from two clay circles (1¹/₂ in. in diameter).

◁ **Optical Illusion** by Haley Hertz
Medallion from a three-color Skinner Blend
(blue to yellow to magenta) rolled into jellyroll
cane; Pavelka peel created embossed, metallic
text effect (2$^{1}/_{2}$ in. by 5 in. by $^{1}/_{2}$ in.).

▽ **Polymer Portfolio** by Scott Mizevitz
Portfolio cover with brass stencil for texture.
Handcrafted faux-gold hardware buffed
with wax metallic finish; ribbon closures
(12 in. by 9 in.).

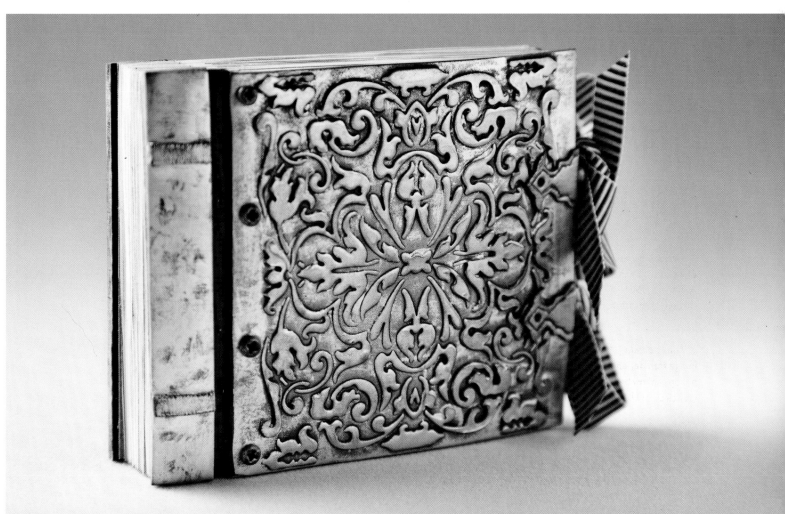

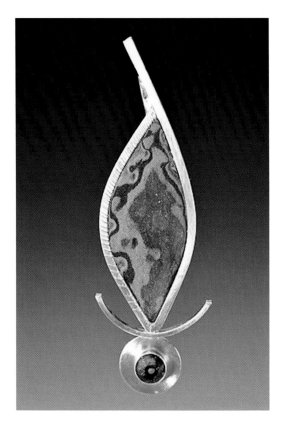

△ **Deco 1** by Helen Wyland-Malchow
Precious metal clay, sterling silver, black onyx
and a Mokumé Gané veneer from handmade
molds (3 in. by 1¹/₂ in. by ¹/₄ in.).

△ **Logo Cane** by Wes Warren
Millefiori caning customized by designer
(5 in. by ¹/₂ in.).

△ **The Love Birds** by Riverdogs
(Deborah Banyas and T.P. Speer)
Hand-formed polymer clay with stuffed cotton
over steel armatures (32 in. by 13 in. by 4 in.).

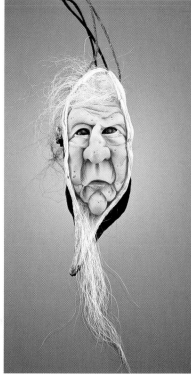

△ *Milkweed Crone*
by Dawn Schiller
Polymer clay with
onyx beads (eyes) and
Tibetan lamb's wool (hair)
(approx. 3 in.).

◁ *Remember When*
by Lisa Pavelka
Straw base purse with image
transfer panels on clay with
molded clay accents, texture
stamped background panels,
and millefiori accents (6 in.
by 8 in. by 3 in.).

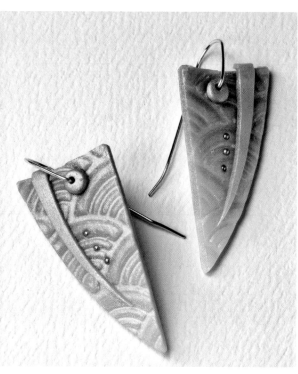

△ *Earrings* by Deborah Brams
Inks and a Skinner Blend for color with Mica Shift technique (1¹/₂ in. by ¹/₂ in.).

△ ▷ *Cosmos* by Julie Picarello
Imprint Mokumé Gané technique accented with painted metal disks and semi-precious gemstones (2 in. by 2¹/₂ in. by ¹/₄ in.).

▷ *Winter Nymph Mask* by Anne Igou
Color blending and stamping techniques over papier-mâché (5¹/₂ in. by 7 in.).

△ **Altered Divas** by Barbara A. McGuire
Transfer, stamping, and embellishment
techniques (2 in. by 4 in.).

◁ **Leafy Lady** by Arbel Shemesh
Gin image transfer method and millefiori
caning (approx. 12 in. by 12 in.).

▽ **Fish Gotta Swim** by Consuela Okdie
Polymer clay embellished with mica and
embossing powders; texture sheets
and Phillips-head screwdriver for texture
effects (8 in. by 10 in.).

△ **Fossil Pendants** by Sophia Lenz
Faux ivory technique with inlay, backfill,
and findings (1 in. by 3 in. by 1/2 in.).

▷ **Jungle Fever-Tiger Necklace** by Janet Pitcher
Complex millefiori caning techniques for clay
beads; copper and natural stone beads
(26 in.; focal bead 2 in. by 2 in.).

△ **Copper Twist Necklace** by Kathi Briefer-Gose
Copper chain mail and Mica Shift twisted square
beads (20 in.).

△ **A River Runs Through It** by Christi Friesen
Clay over glass jar, which was removed after
baking; beads and pearls wired into raw
clay; armature wire inside reeds (7 in. by
8 in. by 5 in.).

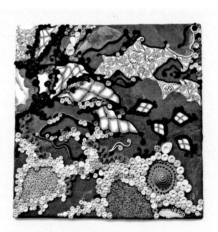

△ **By the Waterside** by Irit Cohen-Irico
Millefiori caning, Skinner Blending, filigree,
texturing, and sculpting over plywood
(12 in. by 12 in.).

▷ **Carnival** by Michele A. Tobler-Sutter
Twelve-color Skinner-Blend stack for Buessler-cut focal bead; wirework with Swarovski, Czech lampwork, and polymer clay beads (necklace: 20 in.; focal bead: 1³/₄ in.).

▷ ▷ **Southwest Sunrise** by Rhonda Garlick
Picarello-inspired Mokumé Gané over textured clay with sterling silver insets; coconut beads (6 ¹/₂ in. by 6 in.).

▷ **Pastels All Around** by Gloria Askin
Beads, pearls, and handmade polymer clay pieces, which employ veneer of caning in a technique developed by artist (21 in. by 2¹/₂ in.).

◁ *Tiger Lily Fairy Collar* by Lynne Ann Schwarzenberg Millefiori caning, sculpting, and texturing techniques (18 in.).

△ *Flip Flop Bracelet* by Audrey Busby
Millefiori cane slices on a layered clay foot form; beading with pearls (straps); jump rings (10 in.).

△ *Butterfly Box* by Robert Wiley
Faux wood with mica technique; marquetry over polymer clay box (6 in. by 4^1/$_2$ in. by 2^1/$_2$ in.).

△ *Ode to da Vinci* by Julie Eakes
Millefiori caning technique (2^1/$_2$ in. by 3 in.).

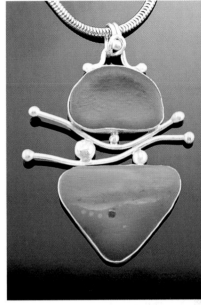

△ *Horizon* by Linda Hirschfield
Skinner Blend, carving, and
backfilling polymer clay with
sheet silver and wire (approx.
1 in. by 2^1/$_2$ in.).

◁ *Polymer Clay Leaf Necklace*
by Carol J. McGovern
Skinner Blending and cutting
(approx. 20 in.).

▷ *Jade Memories* by Gloria Askin
Pearls and flat polymer clay beads with a
veneer of caning using techniques developed
by artist; focal bead Chinese carved jadeite,
fine silver (21 in. x 2¹/₂ in.).

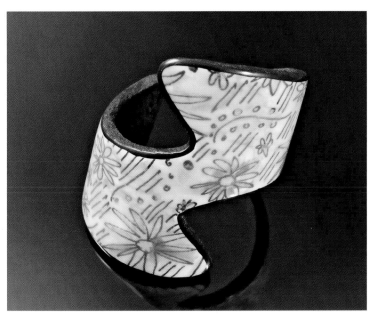

◁ *Flower Garden Cuff Bracelet* by Bettina Welker
Transfer techniques with veneering applied to handmade aluminum bracelet blank ($2^3/_4$ in. by $2^1/_2$ in.).

▽ *Leafy Garden* by Arbel Shemesh
Polymer clay necklace using millefiori caning method; with earrings (12 in. by 12 in.).

▷ **The Healing Ride** by Sophia Lenz
Bottle covered with lightweight Sculpey,
extruded cane pattern for saddle and scarves
(13 in.).

▽ **Flower Necklace** by Bettina Welker
Metal leaf, alcohol inks, and translucent clay for
petals (6 in. by 5 1/8 in. by 1/8 in.).

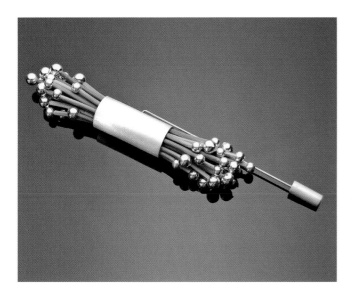

△ **Sticks and Clusters Brooch** by Bettina Welker
Fabricated sterling silver tube setting filled with
extruded sticks from polymer clay (4 in. by 3/4 in.
by 3/4 in.).

△▷ **Nudi Branch** by Melanie West
Bangle from hand-formed armature carved
then laminated with polymer clay millefiori
(5 in. by 5 in. by 1 in.).

▷ **Card Holder** by Lisa Pavelka
Surface and embossed stamping methods; image
transfer to clay, millefiori accents; and mixed
media surface embellishment (2 1/2 in. by 3 3/4 in.).

△ *Japanese Inro Purse* by Haley Hertz
Black clay textured with rubber stamp then painted
with metallic acrylic paints. Antiqued images are
stamped onto layers of ivory clay mixed with silver
leaf and stained with pigment inks. Over cardboard
armature (3$\frac{1}{4}$ in. by 5 in. by $\frac{1}{2}$ in.).

△▷ *Marquetry Necklace* by Robert Wiley
Faux wood made using mica technique inlaid
using marquetry (5$\frac{1}{2}$ in. by 4 in. by $\frac{1}{4}$ in.).

▷ *Man in the Middle* by Lisa Pavelka
Faux ivory overlay, molding, and antiquing.
Clay face set in Art Clay Silver ivy leaf frame
(1$\frac{1}{4}$ in. by 1$\frac{3}{4}$ in.).

△ **Altered Art Clock** by Michelle Herren
Black, ivory, jade, and red polymer clay tile stamped
and antiqued with acrylic paint then sanded to reveal
raised images beneath (8 in. by 8 in. by 1¹/₂ in.).

◁ **Hanging Out** by Christi Friesen
Polymer clay applied to armature of glass jars
and wire; beads wired into clay and, after baking,
strung onto wire for branches and around base.
(12 in. by 6 in. by 6 in.)

▽ **Vesna** by Nevenka Sabo
Necklace from seed beads (8 strings) and round,
hand-shaped polymer clay beads employing a
layering canework technique (22 in., polymer
beads 2 in. and 1 in. in diameter).

APPENDIX I

Troubleshooting for Polymer Clay

Even though polymer clay is a relatively easy medium to learn and master, it's not uncommon to encounter some difficulties as you work with the material. I've included tips and tricks throughout the book to make working with clay easier. Knowing the details that can help prevent or correct problems can make all the difference in ensuring that working with polymer clay is an enjoyable and relaxing experience.

As you work with clay, you'll discover shortcuts and methods for dealing with issues as they arise. These are the "aha" moments, moments that can be deeply satisfying. This section is devoted to helping you keep clear of common mistakes and avoid them altogether. As a columnist for *PolymerCAFÉ Magazine*, I deal with readers' questions every day. What I don't know through decades of clay experience, I research. Some of this knowledge is universal, while some is based on personal discovery.

Here are a few last thoughts that address common situations that arise with polymer clay work. Many other solutions to general problems appear in related chapters throughout the book.

Air Bubbles in Uncured Clay

Air bubbles occurring in raw clay are usually the result of improper conditioning or reconstitution of clay scraps. The best way to combine clay scraps is to gather them loosely and roll them through a large setting on the pasta machine repeatedly until they are combined in a solid sheet. Always roll the clay with the fold at the bottom or to the side. Rolling with the fold at the top can also introduce air.

Multiple folding of thin sheets of clay to thicken them can introduce air, as well. To thicken thin sheets of clay, fold them in half and roll through the previous thickest setting, repeating until you've gradually worked the sheet back to the largest setting.

Large air bubbles can be pierced with a needle tool or sliced with the tip of a craft knife. Smooth the holes or gashes with your fingers or reroll the clay through the pasta machine until smooth and unblemished.

If a large amount of tiny air bubbles appears, gradually roll the clay down to the fifth- or sixth-largest setting of the pasta machine. Hand-stretch the clay as far as you can until it begins to tear. As you do this, you'll notice the bubbles appearing as lighter-colored streaks as they break. Fold the clay in half and reroll on a thin setting, repeating until the bubbles have all disappeared.

Air Pockets in Baked Clay

Air pockets can sometimes occur between baked layers of clay or between the clay and the surface it's covering. To remedy this situation, apply pressure to the raised area for several minutes while the clay is still warm from the oven. Use an oven mitt or the flat backing of a rubber texture sheet while holding the clay down until the clay has cooled (several minutes). This usually will reshape the clay and allow it to remain flat after cooling.

If the air pocket or small bubbles remain after doing this, heat the clay again for a few minutes. With a small needle or the tip of a craft knife, pierce the bubble immediately after taking the clay out of the oven. If possible, make the slit or piercing somewhere inconspicuous. Apply pressure over the bubble with an oven mitt or texture stamp to protect your hands while the clay cools.

In a worst-case scenario where you can't fix a raised air pocket after baking, consider this an opportunity for embellishment. One of the beautiful things about clay is that it can be baked repeatedly. Cover the trouble spot with a clay embellishment. It may become the highlight of your work.

Blade Problems

You may find that you get blurred or drag lines through clay canes or striped loaves when you slice. This is the result of debris on the blade. It might be glue or small pieces of clay. Clean and sharpen your blades following the section on Blades and Knives | see TOOLS AND ACCESSORIES chapter 2, page 23 |. Cleaning your blade frequently while you work will help eliminate many blade issues. Once you can see notches in the bottom of your blade, it's time to dispose of it.

Burning or Discoloration

Clay can experience a change of color, known as color shift, while baking. If properly baked, this difference shouldn't be at all noticeable. Oftentimes, someone will say they know their oven is set to the right temperature, but their clay burns or scorches within minutes of putting it into the oven. This is either a case of failing to preheat the oven or having clay too close

(closer than 2 in. to 3 in.) to a heating element or sidewall.

Always preheat your oven and use an oven thermometer. This is the only way you can ensure proper baking. The general rule of thumb is to bake 15 to 20 minutes for every ¼ in. of clay thickness. You cannot technically overbake clay if following these basic steps. I sometimes bake for hours or bake a piece as many as 10 times to complete a project. Of course, when multiple baking is called for, I only heat-set the clay for 5 to 10 minutes between steps, allowing the final baking to go for at least 20 minutes for every ¼ in. of thickness, based on the thickest portion of my clay.

Clay Conditioning

Polymer clay that won't condition to a workable consistency, no matter how much you knead or roll it, might need to have some translucent or liquid clay added to it. When adding liquid polymer as a softening agent, use only a few drops at a time. Also try warming the clay on a heated (not hot) tile or bag of rice that's been microwaved for 30 to 45 seconds.

The best way to condition crumbly clay is by repeatedly folding and rolling with an acrylic rod over a work tile. Using a pasta machine to condition it can create contamination problems with other colors of clay. This situation can persist for quite some time.

If the clay still won't condition regardless of what you do, it has probably begun curing due to improper storage and exposure to heat. You can crush or

crumble this clay for use as inclusions in translucent and light-colored clays.

Cracked Clay

Cracks can form in clay for a variety of reasons; some of these include working with clay that isn't properly conditioned or compressed, baking at excessively high temperatures, or baking on a surface that expands a great deal when heated (such as wood).

First, pay close attention to properly conditioning clay. Next, make sure that your oven has been preheated and you are using an oven thermometer. If the problem persists, it could mean your thermometer is broken or defective.

When baking over an expanding material like wood, bake the wood two times before adding decorative clay. The first time allows the wood to expand as much as possible. This seasons the wood, preventing it from expanding as much with future baking. Second, brush the wood with a layer of liquid clay and bake. This acts as a primer and makes it easier to add a clay veneer or accents using bonder glue.

To deal with cracks in clay, try the following:

• Backfill the cracks with Rub 'n Buff, a wax-based acrylic patina, or highlight the cracks with acrylic paint. Even if a dramatic, aged affect wasn't intended, this can be a surprisingly attractive enhancement to your work. Wipe away the excess paint with a baby wipe once it's spread over the clay and into the cracks.

- If color remains on the exterior clay surrounding the cracks, it can be removed by wiping repeatedly with a clean cloth or sanding lightly with a high-grit wet-dry sandpaper (1,000 grit or higher).

- Another option for a less visible repair is to backfill the crack with clay of the same color while the clay is still warm from the oven. The piece should be slightly cooled before handling. Press thin slivers of clay cut from a tiny snake and press these down into the cracks. Use the tip of the knife to scrape off the excess clay. Once the cracks are filled, rebake the piece for 10 to 15 minutes to cure the clay. Follow with a light sanding as needed.

Outdoor Use

Baked polymer clay is colorfast and generally very durable, but it is not meant for prolonged outdoor exposure. I have created many pieces for outdoor use, and some have held up incredibly well, while others have not. Much of clay's durability for outdoor use depends on factors such as exposure to harsh conditions, including heat, moisture, and UV exposure. Understand that polymer clay work that is used outdoors and exposed to prolonged harsh conditions may only last a year or two.

I have used clay around a license plate frame that, after six years, contin-ues to hold up well. Also, I've enjoyed a mosaic house number sign that has held up for many years. This doesn't get much direct sunlight, which I credit for its longevity.

Years ago, I also covered the entire back door of a minivan as an alternative to auto body repair. This held up beautifully for the two-and-a-half years I continued to drive this vehicle. Knowing that clay may or may not hold up well outdoors is an important factor when considering whether your time and resources are worth the effort of the limited enjoyment you derive.

Pasta Machine Problems

- If clay consistently sticks to the rollers on the thinnest settings, this indicates that the guide blades are damaged, which is often due to repeatedly forcing too much clay through the machine. It's best not to roll clay that is more than double the thickness of any setting. The machine may still be fine for use on larger settings.

- Use the tip of a latex glove or water balloon on the end of the pasta machine handle to prevent it from slipping out while working.

- Large C-clamps work best for attaching pasta machines to a variety of surfaces. The clamp that comes with the machine won't fit on many tables. Use two clamps if possible to stabilize the machine. The larger the clamps, the better chance you can attach it to any table. The deeper the clamps, the less vibration you will have when rolling.

Surface Contamination

Working with white and light-colored clays can be very challenging. Regardless of how clean you keep your machine and work area, tiny bits of clay have a way of showing up on the surface of baked projects regardless of the care you take.

Do not try to shave or cut contaminated areas out of clay if the imperfection is minor. This will just create a deviation in the surface that is unsightly. Rather, scrape the surface with the flat edge of a craft knife until you "erase" the surface contamination after baking. In most cases, this will not leave any noticeable change in the surface except the absence of the contamination.

When a lighter color of clay has contaminated a darker area of baked clay, touch up the area with an alcohol or permanent marker that matches the color you are correcting. Another option is to use a tiny amount of acrylic paint. When all else fails, embellish the area with another clay accent or finding, then rebake.

Wrong-Sized Holes

When creating a hole in a bead, button, or other project, you may find that you have a hole that is too big. To fix an overlarge hole, pack the opening in baked clay with the same color, rebake, and redrill a smaller hole with a skewer or needle tool.

APPENDIX II

Glossary of Polymer Clay Terms

Acid free (also see Lignin free): This is a term of relevance to paper artists and archivers. The acid level is determined by a pH range of 7.0 to 9.0. Acid-containing materials can weaken or discolor paper over time as well as deteriorate cellulose-based materials. Polymer clay is acid free and archival safe for scrapbooking.

Antiquing: The process of creating an aged look on clay. This can be done using pigment powders, paints, and Rub 'n Buff after baking. An application is made on the baked clay and the excess is wiped or lightly sanded away to create an aged or distressed patina.

Armature: A foundation or framework under clay built for sculptural purposes. It is used to add strength and reduce the amount of clay needed to form a piece that otherwise may be heavier. Wire, aluminum foil, or other materials can be used to create an armature.

Backfill: This is the process of filling crevices in clay with other clays (solid or liquid), paints, or other clay-compatible media. It is a means of achieving looks including intarsia inlay, mosaic, cloisonné, and other enameling methods.

Bead roller: A device for rolling various sized and shaped beads with uniform consistency. The best known and most widely available are patented designs developed by Gale and Sue Lee of Poly-Tools and distributed by AMACO.

Bezel setting: Typically a metal foundation with thin sidewalls designed to frame clay work. Backfilling is the most common technique used with a bezel setting. Commercial settings are available. Recycling old costume jewelry for settings is another fun alternative. Polymer clay bezels can be fabricated to imitate this treatment.

Brayer: This is both a verb and a noun. To brayer means to roll a cylindrical object (usually an acrylic or metal rod) over the clay for the purposes of flattening, smoothing, or impressing against a texture plate to create texture. As a noun, a brayer is a roller with a handle. Brayers are usually acrylic, rubber, silicone, or wood.

Buffing wheel: A polishing wheel made from muslin, wool, cotton, or felt. This is typically attached to a rotating spindle on a bench grinder, lathe, or rotary tool and is used after sanding to buff and polish clay to a glasslike finish. An adapted version can be made using a wool buffing "bonnet" tied over a sanding plate made for a hand drill.

Bull's-eye (see Millefiori): This is a millefiori term for any clay color wrapped in another color. It can refer to a single cane (rod) of clay wrapped in a single clay sheet of another color, or multiple layers of clay wrapped around a central clay core, just as a traditional bull's-eye target might appear.

Burnish: This means to rub. It is used to attach items including foils, leafing, and transfers onto a clay surface. It is typically done with the fingers, but it can also be accomplished with a stiff plastic card or bone folder, depending on the desired outcome.

Cabochon: Also referred to as a "cab." It's the formation (by hand or mold) of a domed piece of clay that can be round, oval, or other shapes. It is flat on the back and typically polished to imitate the look of stone cabochons.

Cane (see Millefiori): A glass-blowing term that, when applied to clay, refers to a colored component of clay or a combination of them to create a pattern assembled in what is known as millefiori.

Chatoyance (see Mica Shift): An optical quality in which an object exhibits a wavy and luminous band of light that appears to glow from within and move when viewed at various angles. This quality is also seen in opals and cat's eyes.

Chroma (see Saturation): Color term that refers to a color's integrity, or a lack of gray or white.

Clay foil: This is a Mylar-backed foil brought to the market by myself (I developed the first Faux Dichroic Glass technique for polymer clay). These foils come in several colors and patterns. They are applied to uncured clay. Heat generated through burnishing, not pressure, makes them adhere. They create a more intense metallic effect on clay than leaf and don't crackle as dramatically when stretched. Foils, like leafing, should be sealed to prevent fading, wearing, or peeling with repeated handling.

Clay gun (see Extruder): An extrusion device that creates clay canes or rods in various shapes and diameter sizes by way of interchangeable disks. Clay guns rely on a plunger to force the clay out of a barrel.

Conditioning: The preparation of clay to reach a workable state. This is typically achieved by one or a combination of the following: kneading, rolling through a pasta machine, and dedicated food-processor granulation. Each brand of clay has its own unique degree of firmness and consistency. Some brands are easier to condition than others.

Cure: The baking of clay to achieve molecular fusion of the molecules, resulting in optimal strength and permanence. Temperatures vary from brand to brand.

Dichroic: A property that causes light to be split up into distinct beams of different wavelengths (colors). It can also mean light rays that have different polarizations. Dichroic glass is a popular type of glass used to make artwork and jewelry. It displays a beautiful iridescent quality throughout a wide spectrum of color.

Dye ink (see Pigment ink): A quick-drying, water-based ink. Dye-based ink may fade over time and with UV exposure. Dye ink is heat-set to a permanent state on polymer clay, but it may lose some intensity during curing. This can be touched up easily with a fine-tip permanent marker.

Embossing powder: A thermographic powder developed for the printing industry and adapted to rubber stamp arts. It can be added to clay as an inclusion or applied to the surface before baking for a stonelike look and other special effects. Some powders are coated and "bloom" during baking, revealing a different color than the exterior coating when heated. Blue can become white in the baking process in some brands. Various grades and coarsenesses can also create a variety of surface textures. Typical rubber stamp applications can be done on baked clay.

Extruder (see Clay gun): A clay gun or device such as a gum paste gun or garlic press, which can be substituted for a clay gun.

Faux: The French word for "false." It is used in many polymer clay techniques to indicate an imitative method. There are many techniques and adaptations for creating faux wood, stained glass, fabric, opal, metal, stone, and more. Polymer clay is the chameleon of artistic mediums. About the only thing that can't be copied is the look of completely transparent glass.

Grit: Refers to the degree of coarseness of sandpaper. The range is extreme, from very coarse to exceedingly fine. Sandpaper can be used to texture or polish baked clay. Not all brands are universal in their actual grit grading. The 600 grit of one brand of paper may be noticeably coarser than the 600 grit of another brand. Typically, polishing clay is done starting with automotive-grade paper from 600 grit, but can start as low as 400 grit.

Guild: A group of individuals who meet for the further development of clay skills and knowledge. Local guilds can be started by anyone and organized in any format that the members mutually agree upon. They can be as small as two people or number in the hundreds of members. Local and regional guilds can be found around the world. Many have their own websites. Some are very organized, and others are more informal. They may require membership dues or have no charge at all to join. The International Polymer Clay Association (www.npcg.org) is an organization that serves the worldwide polymer clay community. Membership is additional to membership in a local guild. The

IPCA is a terrific resource for product information, techniques, education, and competitive opportunities. They serve as a gateway to people who have varied interests in the medium.

Hue: Refers to the modification of a basic color.

Image transfer: A means of transferring photos or artwork onto polymer clay. Various methods for achieving this include toner-based copy transfer, which can be done in black and white or tinted by hand with pastels, chalks, or colored pencils. It can also be done using liquid clays. The easiest method for image transfer directly onto clay is inkjet, preprinted, or customizable transfer medium. Developed for the clay market by Lisa Pavelka, it can also be used on other crafting surfaces.

Inclusion: Any ingredient that is added to clay to create a special effect. Most often inclusions are added into translucent or light-colored clays. Items often used for this purpose include glitter, embossing powder, spices, fibers, ground crayon, metal leafing, and more.

Jelly roll (see Millefiori): One of the simplest and most basic millefiori canes. It is two or more colors of clay rolled into sheets, stacked, and rolled just like a jelly roll cake to form a swirl pattern. More complex versions can be created with wedged sheets, color gradients, and manipulated sheets (including striped, foiled, and textured sheets).

Leafing: Thin sheets of metal traditionally used to gild picture frames, illuminate manuscripts, and embellish walls, ceilings, paintings, and frescos. Most metal leaf that is used for crafting is known as composite leaf. This is metal leaf that appears to be gold, silver, or copper, but is tinted metal such as aluminum. It comes in sheets thinner than paper.

Real gold leaf and other precious metal leafing is typically hundreds of times more expensive per sheet than composite leaf. It can be applied to uncured clay and has a dramatic crackle effect when stretched. Leafed clay, especially anything that will be handled, should be sealed with a thin layer of liquid clay or other compatible sealant to prevent fading, tarnishing, or peeling. Unlike clay foil, leaf comes in a limited number of colors and effects.

Lignin free (see Acid free): Lignin is an organic component found in the cell walls of plants that can be a factor in the deterioration of paper. Lignin, like acid, is harmful to the lifespan of paper and photographs. Polymer clay is lignin free and archival safe.

Liquid clay: Polymer clay in liquid form. It can be applied to seal foils, leafing, powders, paints, and embellishments onto clay. It can also be used to attach clay to clay before curing. Additives including dye, paint, and powders can be mixed into liquid clay to use as a heat-curable paint and surface treatment. Marbling effects with liquid clay mixed with more opacity can be achieved by swirling multiple colors with a pin or needle tool. Liquid clay, when applied thickly enough, is self-leveling. It can even be used as a transfer medium. All liquid clays appear translucent when in the bottle, but they are typically transparent in nature when applied, unless unusually thick layers are used.

Loaf: A stack of layered or striped clays assembled in the form of a square or rectangular. These are assembled to create millefiori, Mokumé Gané, and striped clay veneers.

Log (see Snake): A component of a cane. It can be shaped as a rod, square, triangle, oval, teardrop, or other sculpted lengths.

Marbling: The mixing of two or more clay colors together without blending into a solid color. This technique creates striations and veins in a random pattern that can mimic the look of stone, marble, or paper. Drawing lines through a sheet of marbleized clay using a skewer or knitting needle can create chevron patterning.

Mica pigment powder: Finely granulated mica particles that have been dyed with pigment. When applied to unbaked clay, they can give an iridescent finish that resembles the look of metal or mother of pearl. While they can be added as an inclusion in clay, it takes quite a bit to get a visible effect.

Mica Shift (see Chatoyance, also Pearlescent): A technique that is unique to polymer clay. It is the manipulation of mica particles in metallic polymer clays. Conditioning in a single direction through a pasta machine will align the particles, which work like tiny mirrors. Once these particles are all facing the same direction, they can be manipulated with the use of a texture stamp, or by cutting and assembling grain against cross-grain to create a ghosted effect.

Impressed metallic clay is shaved until smooth, leaving a ghosted effect. This is actually a type of "bruising of the clay." Both methods used to create a mica shift work like a hologram. The clay appears to have texture, but is in fact flat and smooth. This effect is enhanced by polishing, which increases the illusion of depth in the pattern. The technical term for the phenomenon that occurs with the Mica Shift technique is *chatoyance*.

Millefiori (see Cane): Derived from the ancient Roman glass-blowing method, it literally means "a thousand flowers" in Italian. It is the formation of patterns or pictures through the combination of canes. These are assembled and compressed together. Slices can be cut from finished canes and applied to clay and other surfaces for a decorative veneer. Individual slices can be layered or assembled to form dimensional or sculptural effects.

Mokumé Gané: Pronounced "mah-ku-may gone-ay," this technique has been adapted from the metalsmithing technique discovered by the 17th-century metalsmith Denbei Shoami. It literally means wood (moku), eye (mé), and metal (gan). The term is often translated as "wood grain metal." It involves creating loaves of clay from thin layers that are stacked and manipulated with the use of texture stamps, tools, or other findings to create holes, hills, and/or ridges. When thinly sliced, the loaf reveals various random patterns of amazing beauty. Applying clay foil or leaf between these thin layers can enhance the effect, especially when layered between translucent clays.

Monochromatic: Refers to all of the hues of a single color (both tints and shades). The resulting look is subtle due to the lack of contrast.

Needle tool: An awl-like tool with a pointed tip, used to pierce texture and pick up clay. It's easy to create needle tools in a variety of lengths and diameters by creating handles for various size needles.

Opaque (see Translucent): Anything that is impenetrable by visible light. It will neither reflect nor emit light.

Pearlescent (see Mica Shift): A term that refers to the shimmer effect found in mica-bearing clay. These microscopic particles reflect light and are a key component in the Mica Shift technique.

Pigment: A dry, pulverized coloring agent that, when suspended in liquid or gel-type mediums, becomes clay, ink, dye, or paint.

Pigment ink (see Dye ink): A heavier-bodied, slower-drying ink. Color saturation on polymer clay tends to be more intense and not as prone to fading during baking or over time. Pigment ink becomes permanent during the curing process for clay.

Plasticizer: A substance that imparts flexibility, softness, and malleability to materials such as polymer clay.

Polymer clay: A nontoxic, man-made modeling material based on PVC composition (polyvinyl chloride). It is made up of thermoplastic resin, plasticizer, and pigment. Unlike earthenware clay, polymer clay contains no water, cures at low temperatures, and has an indefinite shelf life when properly stored.

Polymer clay properties vary from brand to brand considerably. It can be baked in a home oven, convection oven, or toaster oven. It is compatible for baking with many materials (that don't burn at 275°F), including paper, wood, cardboard, papier-mâché, metal, glass, crystal, pearls, feathers, fabric, and some plastics. It can be baked repeatedly. Afterward, it can be drilled, sanded, painted, and carved.

Reduction: A variety of techniques used to compress and reduce a cane in size. A combination of squeezing, stretching, pulling, and rolling are used to lengthen a cane. A cane, when properly compacted and reduced, will maintain the integrity of its design with little or no distortion.

Release agent: Any substance that prevents clay from sticking either to itself or other materials like texture stamps, molds, punches, or rollers. A variety of materials can be used as release agents, including cornstarch (which can leave a residue) and water (which has a tendency to bead). I recommend a silicon automotive protectant spray such as STP Son-of-a-Gun!® or Armor All®, found at any automotive supply store or most discount stores.

When working with a release agent like automotive protectant spray, it's best to spray onto the clay and not the items it comes in contact with. Spaying a stamp, for example, is hit or miss since the spray probably won't reach all the crevices. A small amount applied directly to the clay and spread with a finger will ensure all of the surface is coated and will release cleanly and easily. Decorative applications of clay foil, leaf, or mica powder can also act as release agents.

Relief: The sculptural method of creating three-dimensional imagery in an almost flat composition. Coins are the best example of how dramatic relief work can be in creating the illusion of depth and dimension in a nearly level plane.

Rope: The twisting of two or more snakes of clay. Clay gun disks extrude clay that, when twisted, appears to be multiple snakes of clay entwined together.

Saturation: The degree of chroma in a color or the purity of a color. It also can refer to the lack of white in a color.

Shade: Refers to the gradation of color as related to its degree of darkness or the amount of black that is added.

Skinner Blend: A technique developed by polymer clay pioneer Judith Skinner in which a color gradient is formed between two or more colors of clay. This innovative and time-saving technique revolutionized polymer clay work. It is a staple component for many projects that involve millefiori caning, backgrounds, and embellishment.

Snake: A length of clay that can be rolled into a round shape or formed into squares, rectangles, teardrops, or triangles.

Temperate manipulation: Polymer clay can be reshaped when necessary because of the presence of air bubbles, pockets, and unexpected curvature of items that may occur when cooling.

If an item needs reshaping, heat it for a few minutes in a 265°F oven. Remove and gently hold down the area that needs reshaping with an oven mitt or rubber texture plate for a few minutes. When the clay cools, it will retain the newly formed shape.

Because even the strongest of clays is soft and somewhat brittle when very warm, this should be done with care. Aggressive bending or attempting to reshape can result in breakage.

Texture plate: Anything that can create a texture on polymer clay. Rubber stamps and plastic rubbing plates are the most commonly used products to create texture in clay. Fabric, wood, sandpaper, screening material, and even the soles of shoes can create wonderful textured effects.

Tone: A term used to refer to the light or dark values of a color.

Translucent: A quality that permits the shining through or passage of light without being transparent. This is the nature of polymer clay without pigment added. A very small amount of colored clay will tint an entire block of translucent clay when mixed into it. When used in very thin applications, it can become nearly transparent.

Transparent: A quality that allows light to pass through a material, leaving images on the other side visible. Transparency is the opposite of opacity.

Value: The relative lightness or darkness of a color.

Vessel: Any type of container, including boxes, canisters, vases, or cups.

Work surface: Many types of surfaces can be used with polymer clay. One of the best is ceramic tile because it is inexpensive, comes in many sizes, is easy to transport, is almost impossible to scratch, and can be baked on. Disposable craft papers or deli sheets are also good to work on, especially when you do not wish your clay to stick to the work surface.

These surfaces can be used for baking on, but only for heavier items, as they will curl when they cool. In a pinch, tempered glass, marble, Formica®, or even parchment paper can be used.

Uncured polymer clay should never be allowed to sit on painted, lacquered, or varnished surfaces. Clay will react to the solvent base of these materials and ruin the finish.

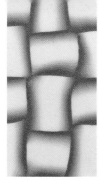

Resource Guide

Further Reading and Educational Resources

Claying Around with Lisa Pavelka
DVD, Lisa Pavelka, 2007; JHB International.

Elegant Gifts with Polymer Clay,
Lisa Pavelka, 2004; North Light Books.

Foundations in Polymer Clay Design,
Barbara A. McGuire, 1999; Krause Publications.

The New Clay Techniques and Approaches to Jewelry Making, Nan Roche, 1992; Flower Valley Press.

Polymer Clay Extravaganza,
Lisa Pavelka, 2000; North Light Books.

Polymer Clay Treasures
DVD, Lisa Pavelka, 2005; PageSage Productions.

Quick and Easy Gifts in Polymer Clay,
Lisa Pavelka, 2005; North Light Books.

Organizations

International Polymer Clay Guild
Website: www.npcg.org
International organization dedicated to polymer clay education.

Periodicals

Art Jewelry
Telephone: 800-533-6644
Website: www.artjewelrymag.com
Magazine devoted to the creation of jewelry, featuring many polymer clay articles.

Bead & Button
Telephone: 800-533-6644
Website: www.beadandbutton.com
Bimonthly magazine showcasing decorative wearables.

Bead Unique™
Telephone: 800-935-3631
Website: www.beaduniquemag.com
Quarterly magazine devoted to beadwork with a regular feature by Lisa Pavelka and other contributing clay artists.

The Crafts Report
Telephone: 800-331-0038
Website: www.craftsreport.com
Monthly magazine devoted to the hobby-for-profit and professional crafter.

Ornament Magazine
Telephone: 800-888-8950
Website: www.ornamentmagazine.com
Five issues yearly, featuring wearable art.

PolymerCAFÉ Magazine
Telephone: 800-458-8237
Website: www.polymercafe.com
Bimonthly magazine devoted to polymer clay art, Lisa Pavelka's Q & A column.

Suppliers

Alumicolor
Telephone: 800-624-9379
Website: www.alumicolor.com
Rulers, measuring tools

American Art Clay Co., Inc. (AMACO)
Telephone: 800-374-1600
Website: www.amaco.com
Polymer clay tools and accessories, Rub 'n Buff, gold leaf, WireForm®, Fun Wire™

Art Institute Glitter, Inc.
Telephone: 877-909-0805
Website: www.artglitter.com

Artbeads.com
Telephone: 866-715-2323
Website: www.artbeads.com
CRYSTALLIZED–*Swarovski Elements* and
jewelry findings

Clearsnap
Telephone: 800-448-4862
Website: www.clearsnap.com
Ancient Page™ stamp inks

EZScreenPrint
Telephone: 520-423-0409
Website: www.ezscreenprint.com
Kits and materials for creating silk
screens for clay

FIMO Clay
Website: www.eberhardfaber.com/
FIMOMain_GB.EBERHARDFABER

Fire Mountain Gems
Telephone: 800-423-2319
Website: www.firemountaingems.com
CRYSTALLIZED–*Swarovski Elements*,
jewelry findings, and tools for clay

Fiskars
Telephone: 866-348-5661
Website: www.fiskarscrafts.com
Craft knives, decorative edge scissors,
and rotary cutters

Golden Artist Colors
Telephone: 800-959-6543
Website: www.goldenpaints.com
Acrylic paints

Hammerhead America
Telephone: 800-261-4772
Website: www.hammerheadamerica.com
Two-part epoxy

Heritage Handcrafts
Telephone: 303-683-0963
Website: www.heritage-handcrafts.com
Brass stencils

Kemper Enterprises
Telephone: 800-388-5367
Website: www.kempertools.com
Kemper pattern cutters, styluses,
and clay tools

Lisa Pavelka
Website: www.lisapavelka.com
Blog: www.lisapavelka.typepad.com
News, workshop, and contact informa-
tion for author

Lisa Pavelka Signature Craft Products
Website: www.lisapavelka.com
Magic-Glos, Texture Plates, Poly Bonder
Glue, Clay Foils, Image Transfers, Border
Molds, Embossing Cutters

Parawire
Telephone: 973-672-0500
Website: www.parawire.com
Coated wire for clay and jewelry making

Pardo Clay (Viva Décor)
Telephone: 215-634-2235
Website: www.screenprintsupply.com/
viva-decor
Polymer clay for jewelry design

Polyform Products
Website: www.sculpey.com
Prēmo! Sculpey, Sculpey III, Translucent
Liquid Sculpey

Polymer Clay Express
Telephone: 800-844-0138
Website: www.polymerclayexpress.com
Polymer clay, tools, premade silk screens,
accessories

Rupert, Gibbon & Spider Inc. (Jacquard)
Telephone: 800-442-0455
Website: www.jacquardproducts.com
Pearl Ex powders

Staedtler
Telephone: 800-776-5544
Website: www.staedtler-usa.com
Fimo Clays, tools

Wilton
Telephone: 800-794-5866
Website: www.wilton.com
Cutters and tools that work with
polymer clay

Websites

Polymer Clay Central
www.polymerclaycentral.com
One of the oldest and most comprehensive polymer clay websites. Filled with
project and product information. Great
resource for polymer clay links.

Polymer Clay Daily
www.polymerclaydaily.com
Cynthia Tinapple's daily site for clay
inspiration and innovations.

Glass Attic
www.glassattic.com
Online encyclopedia of polymer
clay knowledge.

Index

Index note: page references in *italics* indicate a photograph; page references in **bold** indicate a drawing.

A
Adhesives and glues, 28, *28, 29*
Anderson, Deborah, *190*
Askin, Gloria, *198, 202*

B
Banyas, Deborah, *192*
Barber pole striping, 141, *141*
Belcher, Judy, 83
Border treatments, 84, *84,* 142, *142*
Brams, Deborah, *194*
Briefer-Gose, Kathi, *197*
Buesseler, Mike, 82
Buffing, 19, *19, 20*
Busby, Audrey, *200*

C
Canes/caning:
    bull's eye, 38, *38,* 39, *39,* 40, *40,* 41
    checkerboard, 56, *56,* 85, *85*
    exact size, 49
    face, *15, 47, 48*
    flower, *46,* 54–55, *55*
    heart, *56,* 57, *57*
    history of, 45
    "invisible," 83
    jelly-roll, 41, *41,* 42, **42,** 51, *51*
    leaf, 52, *52,* 53, *53,* 54, *54*
    mirror canes, 57, 59, *59,* 164, *164,* 165, *165,*
        166, *166,* 167, *167*

    packing, 48–49, *49*
    reconditioning, 16
    reducing, 16, 47, 49, *49,* 50, *50*
    scrap clay, 60, *60,* 61, *61*
    shapes, 48–49, 50, *50*
    slicing, 50, *50*
    smoosh canes, 57, *57,* 58, *58,* 59, *59*
    storing, *15,* 16
    striped jelly roll, 51, *51*
    tie-dye canes, 57, *57,* 58, *58,* 59, *59*
    See also Millefiori caning
Carving, *124,* 129, *129*
Cernit, 8
Chalk, 34
Cinnabar, faux, 108, *108*
Cohen-Irico, Irit, *197*
Color recipes:
    chip charts, 18, *18,* 19, 147, *147*
    inclusions, 19, 32–33, *33,* 34, *34,* 35, *35,*
        146, *146,* 147, *147*
Crackle effect, 104, *104,* 105, *105*
Creping technique, 142, *142*
Cutter boxes, 135, *135,* 136, *136*

D
Deli paper, 12, 25, 71, *71,* 94, *94,* 95

E
Eakes, Julie, *200*
Eberhard Faber, 7, 8, *9*
Embossing powders, 33, 97, *97,* 146, *146,* 147, *147*

F
Faux Dichroic glass, 93, 172, *172,* 173, ***173,***
    174, *174,* 175, *175*
Faux Dichroic Shield Pendant project, 172,
    172, 173, ***173,*** 174, *174,* 175, *175*
Faux effects, *100,* 101–109, 172–75
Fibers, 34, *34,* 35, *35,* 147, *147*
FIMO clays and products, 7, 8, *9,* 10, *10,* 11, 12,
    32, 33, 35
Finishing:
    buffing, 19, *19,* 20
    polishing, 19, *19*
    sanding, 19, *19,* 20
    sealers and glosses, 35, 93
Flowers, 54–55, *55,* 133, *133,* 134, *134*
Foiling effects, *90, 91,* 93–99
    applying foil, 94, *94,* 95, 151, *151*
    clay compatible, 34, 35, 93, *93,* 94
    Pavelka Peel, 98, *98,* 99, *99*
    resists, 97, *97,* 98, *98,* 99, 99
    sealing, 11
    textures and dimensions, 96, *96*
Ford, David, 37
Forlano, Steven, 37
Friesen, Christi, *197, 207*

G
Gallery of polymer clay art, *188,* 189–207
Garlick, Rhonda, *198*
Gibson, Gwen, 144
Glitter, 11, 33, 38, 146, *146*
Glues and adhesives, 28, *28,* 29
Gradient canes and loaves, 38, 43, *43,* 56, *56,*
    57, *57*

Granular surface treatments, 146, *146*, 147, *147*

H

Herren, Michelle, *207*
Hertz, Haley, *191, 206*
Hirschfield, Linda, *201*
Hollow forms, 130, *130*, 131, *131*
Hughes, Victoria, 101

I

Igou, Anne, 115, *194*
Image transfers, 34, *35, 62,* 63–71
    coloring toner transfers, 70, *70*
    custom inkjet, 66, *66,* 67
    deli paper, 71, *71*
    Inro Amulet project, 176, *176,* 177, *177,* 178, *178,* 179, *179,* 180, *180,* 181, *181*
    liquid clay, 10, 68, *68,* 69
    preprinted waterslide, 67
    protecting and sealing, 71
    stamping, 67, *67*
    tone-based, 69, *69,* 70, *70*
    waterslide transfers, 64, *64,* 65, *65,* 67
Inclusions, 19, 32–33, *33,* 34, *34,* 35, *35,* 146, *146,* 147, *147*
Ivory, faux, 106, *106,* 107, *107*

J

Jacquard Pearl Ex, 32, 33, *33*
Jewelry:
    coiled tube attachments, 152–53, *153*
    fancy or coil-wrapped loops, 157, *157*
    findings, 154, *154*
    fold-over bails, *152,* 154, *154*
    forming eye pins, 155–56, *156,* 157, *157*
    jump rings, 155, *155*
    suspending options, 132, *132,* 152, *152*
    tools and skills, 154, *154,* 155, *155,* 156, *156,* 157, *157*
Junk or scrap canes, 60, *60,* 61, *61*

K

Kato Polyclay and products, *9,* 10, *10,* 11
Kemper Tools, 30, *30*
Krahula, Rebecca, 69
Krause, Jim, 17

L

Leaching, 12–13
Lee, Gale, 28
Lee, Sue, 28
Lentils, 130, *130*
Lenz, Sophia, *196, 204*
Liquid clay:
    adding color, 10
    applications, 10, *10,* 11
    as adhesive, 29
    cleaning, 11
    curing, 11
    dedicated brushes, 11, 68
    dichroic glass look, 93
    transfers, 68, *68,* 69
Loaves, gradient, 43, *43*

M

Magic-Glos, 35, 93
Magic-Mirror: Millefiori-tiled project, 164, *164,* 165, *165,* 166, *166,* 167, *167*
Makin's Clay, *26*
Marbling, 140, *140*
McGovern, Carol J., *201*
McGuire, Barbara A., *195*
Metal leafing, 11, 34, *35,* 90, 91, 92, *92,* 93, 152, *152*
Metallic clays, 82, 83, *83*
Mica powders, 11, 32–33, *33*
Mica Shift effects, 32, *80,* 81–89
    chatoyancy, 82–83
    checkerboard cane, 85, *85*
    embossing, 86, *86,* 122–23, *123*
    mosaic, 87, *87*
    patterned overlays, 84, *84*
    polishing, 86
    ribbons, 84, *84*
    striped snakes, 84, *84*
    surface and border treatments, 84, *84*
    wood grain, 88, *88,* 89, *89*
Millefiori caning, 10, *44,* 45–61
    flower canes, 54–55, *55*
    gradient checkerboard, 56, *56*
    gradient heart canes, 56, 57, *57*
    history of, 45–46
    junk or scrap clay canes, 60, *60,* 61, *61*
    leaf canes, 52, *52,* 53, *53,* 54, *54*

Magic-Mirror tiled project, 164, *164,* 165, *165,* 166, *166,* 167, *167*
    mirror canes, 57, 59, *59,* 164, *164,* 165, *165,* 166, *166,* 167, *167*
    packing, 48–49
    reducing, 49–50
    shapes, 48–49
    slicing, 48, 50, *50*
    smoosh canes, 57, *57,* 58, *58,* 59, *59*
    storing, *15,* 16, 48
    striped jelly roll, 51, *51*
    working in exact size, 49
    See also Canes/caning
Mizevitz, Scott, 191
Mokumé Gané, 32, *72,* 73–78, *79*
    bladed, 76, *76*
    folded, 78, *78*
    indented, 77, *77*
    polishing, 75
    rolled, 78, *79*
    stamping, 74, *74,* 75, *75*
    stencil, 143, *143*
Mosaics, 125–26, *126,* 127, *127,* 128, *128*
Muslin jeweler's buffing wheels, *19, 20*

O

Okdie, Consuela, *196*
Opal, faux, 102, *102*

P

Pardo clay, 8, *9,* 10, 12
Pasta machine conditioning, 12, 13, 25, *25,* 26, 38–39, *39,* 40, *40,* 41, *41,* 210
Pavelka Peel, 98, *98,* 99, *99*
Picarello, Julie, *194*
Pillow forms, 131, *131*
Pitcher, Janet, *196*
Polishing, 19, *19*
Polymer: The Chameleon Clay (Hughes), 101
Polymer clay art, gallery of, *188,* 189–207
Polymer clay essentials:
    baking, 7, 12, *12,* 13–14, 48, 209
    clay glossary and terms, 211–15
    cleaning, 11, 12, 13
    color basics, 2, 16, *16,* 17, *17*
    color recipes and chip charts, 18, *18,* 19, 147, *147*